CONVERSION
as a Way of Life

CONVERSION
as a Way of Life

ADVICE
FROM
THE
EPISTLES

James J. Bacik

Foreword by
Donald Senior, CP

Paulist Press
New York / Mahwah, NJ

Cover image by Liia Chevnenko / Shutterstock.com
Cover and book design by Lynn Else

Library of Congress Cataloging-in-Publication Data
Names: Bacik, James J., 1936– author.
Title: Conversion as a way of life : advice from the Epistles / James J. Bacik ; foreword by Donald Senior, C.P.
Description: New York / Mahwah, NJ : Paulist Press, 2021. | Summary: "Using principles derived from theologian Bernard Lonergan, James Bacik explores the facets of conversion found in the letters of the New Testament in a down-to-earth way. Includes practical examples and action suggestions"— Provided by publisher.
Identifiers: LCCN 2020027712 (print) | LCCN 2020027713 (ebook) | ISBN 9780809155361 (paperback) | ISBN 9781587689321 (ebook)
Subjects: LCSH: Conversion--Biblical teaching. | Bible. Epistles--Criticism, interpretation, etc. | Lonergan, Bernard J. F. | Catholic Church—Doctrines.
Classification: LCC BS2635.6.C59 B33 2021 (print) | LCC BS2635.6.C59 (ebook) | DDC 248.2/4--dc23
LC record available at https://lccn.loc.gov/2020027712
LC ebook record available at https://lccn.loc.gov/2020027713

ISBN 978-0-8091-5536-1 (paperback)
ISBN 978-1-58768-932-1 (e-book)

Published by Paulist Press
997 Macarthur Boulevard
Mahwah, New Jersey 07430
www.paulistpress.com

Printed and bound in the
United States of America

In memory of Fr. Bernard J. Boff (1932–2013), my seminary classmate, longtime friend, fellow priest, and enduring inspiration who steadfastly witnessed for justice around the world; in the central city of Toledo; Selma, Alabama; Resurrection City, Washington, DC; and Hwange, Zimbabwe. A dedicated Catholic priest with a Cruciform Heart, who offered up his decade-long battle with Parkinson's disease for the cause of justice and the glory of the Gracious Mystery.

Contents

Foreword

The older I get (and I do...) the more I appreciate the genuine humanity and practical wisdom of Paul the Apostle. Paul wore his heart on his sleeve and could be deeply hurt by the opposition he experienced from his fellow Christians who were worried that his brand of the gospel was too radical when it came to welcoming Gentiles into the Church. The catalogue of the sufferings Paul experienced in the course of his ministry expressed in 2 Corinthians 11:24–29 reveals a man of great passion and enduring commitment:

> Five times at the hands of the Jews I received forty lashes minus one. Three times I was beaten with rods, once I was stoned, three times I was shipwrecked, I passed a night and a day on the deep; on frequent journeys, in dangers from rivers, dangers from robbers, dangers from my own race, dangers from Gentiles, dangers in the city, dangers in the wilderness, dangers at sea, dangers among false brothers; in toil and hardship, through many sleepless nights, through hunger and thirst, through frequent fastings, through cold

and exposure. And apart from these things, there is the daily pressure upon me of my anxiety for all the churches. Who is weak, and I am not weak?

At the same time, when Paul reflected on the beauty of Christ and the promise of life with God, his prose could soar, as in the concluding portion of chapter 8 of his letter to the Romans: "What will separate us from the love of Christ?... For I am convinced that neither death, nor life, nor angels, nor principalities, nor present things, nor future things, nor powers, nor height, nor depth, nor any other creature will be able to separate us from the love of God in Christ Jesus our Lord" (Rom 8:35, 38–39).

Paul was, at the same time, a passionate follower of Christ, a thoughtful and deeply intelligent thinker, and a man driven by his mission to bring the gospel to the world. His letters were retained by the early Christian communities that received them and quickly became a major part of the sacred writings of Early Christianity.

That combination of intelligent reflection, practical pastoral wisdom, and deep passionate commitment characterizes the contents of this book and is a hallmark of its author. I first met Fr. Jim Bacik many years ago when invited by him to speak at Corpus Christi, the campus parish for the University of Toledo where he served as an extraordinary pastor. Under Jim's exceptional leadership it became a model of what a vibrant Catholic community can be. It was a spiritual oasis for the students and also a magnet for the university's faculty and neighbors who drew solid nourishment from the quality of its worship, the eloquence of the pastor's preaching, and the rich fare of lectures and programs that represented the best of Catholic tradition.

Fr. Jim's pastoral skill went side by side with his strong theological skill, honed by his spiritual kinship with the great Catholic theologian and champion of Vatican II, Karl Rahner, SJ. That expertise has led to a long and distinguished list of books and articles published on both a scholarly and popular level and earned Fr. Jim Bacik the deserved reputation as one of the United States' most distinguished and well-known theologians.

This latest book draws on the deep reservoirs of Jim Bacik's pastoral and theological skills. Organized according to the various facets of "conversion" elaborated by another great theologian, Bernard Lonergan, SJ, it provides succinct and luminous reflections on passages from Paul's letters and other New Testament letters. Each of these New Testament texts were, in fact, intended to give pastoral and theological guidance to the early Christians as they pioneered how to follow Jesus in the context of the first-century Greco-Roman world. The format of the unique set of reflections provided here enables the reader to learn the content of the biblical passage under consideration, its meaning for contemporary Christian life, and specific examples of how the biblical message can change our lives. Just skimming through the titles of these 139 meditations reveals the wide range and immediate relevance of these reflections for those striving to lead an authentic Christian life in today's world.

Spirituality is a popular word these days...employed by management gurus, championed by SoulCycle leaders, and offered online by a host of life coaches. Hopefully such efforts do good for those searching for meaning in their lives. More rare and urgently needed, though, is authentic Catholic and Christian spirituality that both draws on a strong biblical and theological foundation and is appreciative of the realities of everyday life. Such is precisely the qualities of this unique and valuable contribution by Fr. Jim Bacik.

Fr. Donald Senior, CP
President Emeritus
Catholic Theological Union
Chicago, Illinois

Preface

The outstanding work on theological method, *Method in Theology* (1972), by the great Canadian Jesuit theologian Bernard Lonergan (1904–84), remains a rich resource for reflection on the spiritual life and personal development. Lonergan, who spent his whole priesthood in the academic world, provides a solid alternative to the superficial and faddish approaches to spirituality so prevalent in contemporary culture.

In general terms, Lonergan identifies five of what he calls "transcendental precepts," or general principles, to guide our spiritual growth:

1. Be attentive by carefully examining the full range of our experience.
2. Be intelligent by cultivating our mental capacities and achieving deeper insights into our experiences.
3. Be reasonable by judging the validity of our insights.
4. Be responsible by acting on our valid insights.
5. Be loving by committing ourselves wholeheartedly to doing God's will.

These precepts guide an integrated ongoing process of moving toward greater spiritual maturity. In this process, sequence can be important; for example, we must understand the consequences of a next step on our spiritual journey before making the decision to take it.

In his book *Method in Theology*, Lonergan uses the notion of "conversion" to present a systematic approach to spiritual growth. Some Catholics are leery of the word *conversion* because they associate it with the sudden, total, once-and-for-all turning from a sinful life to acceptance of Christ, commonly described by evangelical Christians. For Lonergan, however, conversion involves a process of expanding our horizons and making progress in the various dimensions of our lives: intellectual, moral, and religious. We are self-transcendent creatures, called to conversion by seeking more knowledge, better values, and deeper love. Conversion is possible in all dimensions of our lives: for example, we can achieve a more mature understanding of our faith, overcome a persistent fault, and improve our prayer life.

Since, according to Lonergan's anthropology, we are at the same time unique individuals and social creatures, conversion is both highly personal and socially significant. For example, new insights can be shared with others; moral transformations can lead to group actions; deeper love of God can lead to more wholehearted participation in eucharistic liturgy. Finally, Lonergan recognizes that conversions can be fragile, subject to reversals and breakdowns. Bias can cloud our understanding of significant issues, selfishness can cause us to choose expediency over principle, and sin can weaken our relationship with God.

For Lonergan, conversions involve achieving higher standpoints (think of climbing a mountain) that reveal broader horizons, which in turn open up new sources of knowledge and new opportunities for love. Sometimes these breakthroughs, which are always gratuitous, unmerited gifts from God, happen quickly and unexpectedly. On other occasions, the higher standpoint and broader horizon come after step-by-step persevering efforts. Furthermore, within a given horizon it is always possible for us to grow spiritually by being more attentive, intelligent, reasonable, responsible, and loving, which is itself part of the overall conversion process.

The practical advice for spiritual growth in this book is derived from passages in the New Testament letters and epistles that are familiar to Christians who follow the common lectionary at regular Sunday worship. In addition to the four Gospels, the Acts of the Apostles, and the concluding Book of Revelation, the New Testament contains twenty-one letters or epistles. Of these, thirteen identify the Apostle Paul as their author. That attribution is generally accepted by scholars as accurate for Romans, 1 and 2 Corinthians, Galatians, Philippians, 1 Thessalonians, and Philemon. These authentic letters follow a general format: a greeting identifying the sender and the recipient, a prayer of thanksgiving, the body of the letter that includes Christian teaching and applications to moral behavior, a discussion of practical matters, and a farewell. This essential connection between what we believe and how we act is especially important for our effort to glean practical advice from the epistles.

Most scholars think Ephesians, Colossians, 2 Thessalonians, and 1 Timothy were written by disciples of Paul after his death. The Letter to the Hebrews does not claim Paul as its author and was written by an unknown author with a different style and vocabulary.

The other seven letters are generally called the "Catholic Epistles" and were addressed to a general audience and not to a particular community. Three of these (1, 2, and 3 John) serve as commentaries on the Fourth Gospel.

The New Testament letters cover more than a half century of the early Jesus movement, ranging from 1 Thessalonians, the earliest book, written around AD 50 (decades before Mark, the earliest Gospel), to 2 Peter, the latest book, possibly composed as late as AD 120. Thus, the letters contain practical advice for changing circumstances over time in the early Church.

In tapping the doctrinal and ethical wisdom of these letters and epistles, it is helpful to identify the common human concerns that were at work centuries ago and are still in place today, although in different forms. For example, the way Paul dealt with divisions in the Corinthian community over social status and special spiritual gifts still speaks to us today as we deal with divisions between liberal and conservative Catholics. The meditations in this book are based on identifying the common human concerns that continue to play a significant role in our lives today and applying the enduring wisdom of the epistles to contemporary situations.

My hope is that these meditations will promote genuine spiritual growth: that the titles will direct readers to topics of interest; that linking the concerns of the epistle writers with the concerns of spiritual searchers today will make the scriptures more relevant; that the frequent repetition of background material in the epistles (when written, by whom, for which audience, for what purpose) will be helpful for persons reading one meditation at a time; that the concrete examples of conversion in each of the meditations will suggest the possibility of spiritual growth for all of us; and that the question at the end will prompt concrete steps forward for individuals on a unique spiritual journey. Authentic conversions are always the work of the Holy Spirit, who guides and facilitates our prayerful, cooperative responses to divine initiatives.

The meditations are arranged according to the types of conversions identified by Bernard Lonergan. The first chapter includes meditations that call for intellectual conversion, understood as a process that makes us lifelong seekers of wisdom, alert to the mysterious depths of human existence.

Chapter 2 invites reflection on specific passages that call for moral conversions that help us live more prudently, justly, temperately, and courageously in the diverse circumstances of our everyday existence.

The third chapter focuses on passages in the epistles that encourage and guide a religious conversion that rejects prevalent cultural idols, such as hedonism, and concentrates on loving God as the originating Source of our spiritual dynamism and the ultimate Goal of our spiritual journey.

The final chapter on Christian conversion draws on epistle passages that explicitly call for deeper commitment to Jesus Christ, who is true God and true man, the parable of God and the archetype of full authentic humanity. These passages invite reflection on the way Christ was perceived by the early Christians and prompt efforts to live his message in the distinctive circumstances of our lives today.

Chapter One

Intellectual Conversion

Bernard Lonergan often insisted that his carefully crafted methodology should not be followed slavishly but should function as a catalyst for creative approaches. With that in mind, let us examine intellectual conversion as a process that sets us on a lifelong quest for wisdom that transcends scientism, with its exclusive reliance on the empirical method, as well as popular spiritualities, with their emphasis on emotion and intuition to the exclusion of reason and logic. Wise persons realize that real learning is not just about gathering information but about making connections, validating insights, and appropriating common wisdom. They seek an integrated understanding of life that combines the theoretical and the practical as well as self-knowledge and care for the common good. They make good dialogue partners in a pluralistic society because they seek truth without pretending to monopolize it. Furthermore, the wise recognize that intelligence is a broader capacity than reason with its narrow focus on logical analysis. They employ intelligence to probe, understand, and judge all aspects of human experience.

Intellectually converted persons are prepared to criticize various forms of anti-intellectualism in our culture, including the distrust of scholarly work and the fundamentalist tendency to denigrate the role of theology in understanding the scriptures. They also are aware of the limitations of intelligence. We are not able to attend to all aspects of experience. Not all of our bright ideas prove to be true or valid. We make mistakes in judgment. Our horizons of understanding are always limited and less inclusive than we think or hope. On many questions we cannot achieve absolute certitude but must rely on converging probability. By wrestling with the great questions of identity, meaning, and purpose, we learn to accept the ultimately mysterious character of human existence and the limits of our own intelligence.

Being converted intellectually involves specific transitions: from being bored, indifferent, inattentive, and stagnant to energetically searching for truth and wisdom; from an uninformed acceptance of our received religion to a more mature understanding of our faith; from a vague curiosity about life to a more systematic effort to examine, understand, and judge all aspects of experience; from habitually rejecting the views of others to entering into dialogue with others in search of a better understanding of the truth.

There are things we can do to stimulate our intelligence and grow in wisdom, ranging from passing over to the standpoint of others in ordinary conversations to doing a close reading of a classic book. The meditations in this chapter can contribute to the ongoing process of intellectual conversion. We can get more out of them by paying attention to the ways we experience the personal concern expressed in the headings, for example, on befriending death. It helps to approach the epistle passages as inspired sources of practical wisdom that can expand our horizon. The concluding question can suggest specific steps toward living as wise persons.

1. PRAYING FOR THE SPIRIT OF WISDOM

In our struggle to maintain perspective and balance in what has been called our "post-truth" society, we do well to make our own the prayer in Ephesians 1:17–23, asking God to give the followers of Jesus a "spirit of wisdom and revelation." "May the eyes of [your] hearts be enlightened" so you may come to a deeper appreciation of the surpassing power of God, the spiritual gifts received from Christ, and the hope engendered by Christian faith. God's great power has been manifested most decisively in raising Christ from the dead and exalting him "at his right hand in the heavens," high above all celestial beings and "every name that is named." The reign of the ascended Christ is universal, extending to all creatures throughout all history. The passage ends with a reminder that Christ is the head of the Church, "which is his body, the fullness of the one who fills all things in every way."

Ephesians makes it clear that the ascension of Christ is not so much about him leaving his disciples as being present to them in a new way, mediating divine power from his position at God's right hand. As members of the Body of Christ, we have access to the Spirit of wisdom who enlightens the eyes of our hearts to perceive God's glory in ordinary situations, to manifest hope in challenging times, and to rely on divine power in our weakness.

Let us imagine individuals who have been blessed with the spirit of wisdom to find new meaning, hope, and strength in their lives. Maria, wife of a physician and a stay-at-home mother of three, was feeling vaguely guilty because she did not have a paying job outside of the home. Enlightened by the Spirit, she came to see her domestic role in a positive light: her vocation in life, her challenge to create a healthy family environment for individuals she loves, her opportunity to develop important skills, her personal path to holiness, and her way of contributing to society.

Joe, a community organizer, was so depressed by our societal ills (income inequality, ongoing racial tensions, apathy about global warming, deteriorating neighborhoods) that he was thinking of quitting his job and finding something that would shield him from all these intractable problems. One Sunday during Mass, he felt the presence of the Spirit urging him to stay the course, to persevere in the cause of justice, to maintain hope that God hears the cries of the poor and oppressed. This experience sent him back to work with renewed confidence that he was doing something worthwhile.

Sue, a grandmother worn out from raising the two young sons of her cocaine-addicted daughter, was feeling burdened with an undeserved and unfair task. After reflecting on the way Mother Teresa cared for unknown Hindus, Sue found new energy by letting go of her resentment and concentrating on loving her two grandsons who depended on her.

How has the gift of the Spirit of wisdom enriched my life?

2. UNDERSTANDING GOD'S POWER

The dark forces in the world can seem overwhelming: terrorism, war, disease, natural disaster, mass shootings, domestic violence, and personal demons. As believers, we naturally turn to God, the omnipotent Lord, for help, but we need to understand the nature and limits of divine power.

Ephesians 1:17–23 can offer some guidance on this challenging task.

This passage, probably written in the 90s by one of Paul's most eloquent disciples, is cast in the form of a prayer, with a series of petitions, asking God for the gift of wisdom, "resulting in knowledge" of the God of our Lord Jesus Christ, the Father of glory. The author prays, "May the eyes of [your] hearts be enlightened" so we may know God's surpassing power and "great might," which gives us hope that we will share in the inheritance of the "holy ones." God's mighty power raised Christ from the dead and seated him at his right hand, where he reigns over all creatures placed "beneath his feet." As head of the Church, his Body, Christ's glory "fills all things in every way." The author of Ephesians, "Paul's best disciple," prays that we will have a deep personal knowledge and appreciation of God's great might, which will inspire and guide our everyday Christian life.

It is important that we have a proper Christian understanding of God's power, which is always informed by divine love. God's omnipotence is not coercive or harsh. It respects the dynamics of the evolving material world and the fundamental freedom of the human beings created in the divine image. Divine power is loving, compassionate, and forgiving, always empowering us to develop our potential and contribute to the common good. We get our best sense of God's power by reflecting on the story of Jesus who trusted his Father's loving power to the point of death that led to his resurrection and ascension to God's right hand. Christ's victory over death reminds us that God is our mighty champion, more powerful than all the dark forces that assail us.

The epistle's prayerful reflection on God's power could serve as good news for many people: those who need hope in their struggle against addictions; those who are tempted to give up on prayer because it is not helping; those who have encountered the scholarly claim that Jesus was a weak, vac-illating figure who put too much emphasis on being meek; those who buy into the myth that guns are the source of power; those tempted to become cynical about the partisan political divide in our country; those fatigued by the heavy burden of caring for the sick and elderly; those weakened by the misconception that the ascended Christ left us alone; those who are at the mercy of powerful social forces; those brought to despair by chronic pain; and those who no longer seek truth and wisdom. We can all benefit from greater trust in God's merciful compassionate power.

What is my own conception of God's power and how could it be refined?

3. UNDERSTANDING OUR FAITH

As Christians, we have a responsibility to work toward a more mature understanding of our faith. In that effort we could make our own the prayer in the first chapter of Ephesians, asking the "Father of glory" for the "spirit of wisdom and revelation resulting in knowledge of him." The author prays, "the eyes of [your] hearts be enlightened" so that we may have a deeper understanding of the hope of our calling, the glory of our inheritance, and the surpassing greatness of God's power. The author goes on to exalt the risen Christ, seated at God's right hand, far above all the choirs of angels, Lord of all things, and head of the Church, his Body.

Our Christian faith is a surpassing gift that calls for a total commitment to practicing it in all aspects of our daily lives. It is not an esoteric wisdom that provides access to God's secrets available only to a select group. Christianity is a complete way of life open to all persons in every age and culture. In its essence, it is not a set of doctrines to be believed or rules to be observed but rather a call to bet our lives on Christ, to follow his example, and to live according to his teaching.

Living the faith is more important than analyzing it. Christian practice is more important than theological interpretation. Nevertheless, there is a proper role for theology, traditionally understood as "faith seeking understanding." Achieving a deeper understanding of our Christian faith can improve our practice of the faith in various ways: helping us answer objections, providing motivation, suggesting new ways of expressing our core beliefs, indicating constructive ways of relating faith convictions to the challenges of everyday life, and expanding our commitment to the cause of justice and peace in the world.

With these perspectives in mind, we can pray to the Father of glory for the Spirit of wisdom, enlighten the eyes of our hearts that we may better understand your call, your glory, and your great might in exalting Christ over all things in every way. We can imagine individuals who responded to this gift of the Spirit of wisdom. A grandmother acquired a copy of the Catholic Catechism so she could look up answers to religious questions frequently posed by her grandchildren. A plumber, limited by a grade school understanding of his faith, attended a lecture on contemporary theology sponsored by his parish that motivated him to gain a more mature knowledge of the Catholic tradition he received from his parents. A parish religious education director, proud of her master's degree in theology, started to put more emphasis on her personal relationship with Christ that enriched her ministry. A parish religion teacher resolved to improve his classes on Christ by doing some serious reading on the topic.

What concrete step could I take to develop a more mature understanding of my faith?

4. BEFRIENDING DEATH

As we contemplate the stark reality of death, in 1 Corinthians 15:54–58 the Apostle Paul assures us that the risen Christ has conquered death, transforming what is corruptible and mortal into what is incorruptible and immortal. Freely interpreting verses from the Hebrew Scripture, Paul writes, "Death is swallowed up in victory. Where, O death, is your victory? Where, O death, is your sting?" The Apostle reminds us to be grateful to God for giving us this victory through Christ and concludes with the admonition, "Be firm, steadfast, always fully devoted to the work of the Lord, knowing that in the Lord your labor is not in vain."

Through death, we move out of our familiar time-space world into a glorified, fulfilled life beyond even our imagining. Our Christian tradition, however, preserves several teachings that help take the sting out of death and nourish our hope. By surrendering ourselves in death, we will live with God forever. By dying with Christ, we will share in his risen life. In heaven, there will be no more pain, no more suffering, no more tears. When we enjoy the gift of the beatific vision, the deepest longings of our hearts and minds will be completely fulfilled. When we share in the heavenly wedding feast, we will know a peace and joy that passes all understanding. Viewing death from the perspective of the resurrection encourages us to live in the moment, making the most of opportunities for spiritual growth and service to others.

The late Cardinal Joseph Bernardin, archbishop of Chicago and leader of the Catholic Common Ground Initiative, serves as a model of a Christian approach to death. In August of 1996, he announced that he was diagnosed with inoperable pancreatic cancer. In an interview with the *New York Times*, he revealed that he grew up with a deep fear of death through cancer because his father died of that dreaded disease. While he was undergoing radiation treatments, he had a long talk with the spiritual writer Henri Nouwen, who advised him to befriend death as a transition to a better life and as a sharing in the death and resurrection of Christ. Befriending death was a gradual process for him. It did not immediately take away all his fears, since there were still times when he woke up at night in tears, but viewing death as a friend did enable him to manage his fears and maintain his confidence in God's love and mercy. The cardinal admitted he did not know what heaven was like and said it was not helpful for him to think about that. He remained steadfast, making good use of his remaining days by ministering to as many as seven hundred cancer patients and their families. Cardinal Bernardin died November 14, 1996, grateful to the end for the gift of tranquility and peace that comes from befriending death.

What can I learn from the example of Cardinal Bernardin?

5. DISCERNING OUR VALUES

It is easy enough to drift through life without giving much thought to our fundamental value system and our personal priority list. The opening chapter of Paul's letter to the Philippians can serve as a wake-up call to those prone to sleepwalking through life (1:4–11). In this passage Paul expresses his deep affection for his converts, who formed the first Christian church in Europe and have, over time, established a reputation for fidelity to the gospel of Christ. He goes on to express his confidence that God will help them to continue to grow as Christians until the day when Christ returns to complete his saving mission, the culminating event that Christians expected soon. The Apostle then offers a prayer for the Philippians that "your love may increase ever more and more in knowledge and every kind of perception to discern what is of value, so that you may be pure and blameless for the day of Christ."

Let us reflect on Paul's advice "to discern what is of value." We can hear this as an invitation to a personal, prayerful self-examination: What is important to me? What attracts my attention? What moves me to action? What inspires me? What gives me hope? What prompts me to make personal sacrifices? What is at the top of my priority list? What determines my spending habits? Christian faith claims that there is a hierarchy of values that provides a theological framework for clarifying our values and moral perspectives for judging our values.

There are numerous ways of articulating fundamental Christian values. In general, biblical faith values love. God loves all human beings unconditionally. Divine love enlightens our minds and guides our decisions. Drawing on the Hebrew Scriptures, Christ instructs us to love God wholeheartedly and to love our neighbors as ourselves. Furthermore, he taught the essential connection between love of God and love of neighbor. His followers understood the essential deceit in claiming to love God while hating neighbors. By the same token, loving our neighbors implies love of God. Christian love can provide an evaluative framework for individuals to reorder their values.

A hardworking advertising executive could decide to put more time and effort into improving her deteriorating marriage. A man consumed with anger at his older sister who cheated him out of his proper share of their parents' estate could forgive her and concentrate on becoming a more spiritually mature person. A happily married woman with three wonderful children who is constantly frustrated and hurt by her parents' criticism of her husband could stop seeking their approval and enjoy the great blessing of a loving husband. A retired businessman who spent years accumulating wealth only to discover that he was spiritually bankrupt could find genuine fulfillment by devoting himself and his money to empowering the poor and less fortunate.

What reordering of my values would be most beneficial for my spiritual development?

6. FINDING MEANING IN DIFFICULT SCRIPTURE TEXTS

Sometimes it is difficult to find personal meaning in the scriptures written long ago in very different circumstances. However, since all the books of the Bible are the inspired word of God, we can often find a personal message by prayerful reflection on difficult texts. Let us consider a rather obscure passage in the Letter to the Hebrews where the unknown author puts words from Psalm 40 into the mouth of Christ as he was entering the world: "Sacrifice and offering you did not desire, but a body you prepared for me; holocausts and sin offerings you took no delight in. Then I said, 'As is written of me in the scroll, Behold, I come to do your will, O God'" (Heb 10:5–7).

The author, writing to Jewish Christians, is showing the superiority of Christ, our high priest, over the Jewish priests, who repeatedly offered animal and food sacrifices to God. Psalm 40 makes the point that God preferred the interior attitude of obedience over external rituals. Along this line, Christ's sacrifice is superior to Jewish sacrificial rites, because he was obedient to the will of God. He did not seek suffering, but his absolute fidelity to his mission to spread the reign of God enraged the powerful and led to his death on the cross. Furthermore, Christ's sacrifice is preeminent because he offered not an animal but his own body. In the incarnation, the son of God became man, body and soul, sharing completely in our human condition, like us in all things but sin, as Hebrews says elsewhere (4:15). He knew bodily pleasure and bodily pain. As a whole person he suffered emotionally and physically the horrible cruelty of torture and crucifixion. While Jewish ritual sacrifices had to be repeated, the sacrificial death and resurrection of Christ is a once-for-all event that makes salvation irrevocably available to all people at all times. As the last verse of the passage says, "we have been consecrated" (Heb 10:10), sanctified, made holy by Christ, who was obedient to the will of God, offering his body, that is his very self, on the cross for our salvation.

Sacred Scripture, as the inspired word of God and as a collection of classic texts, has a fuller meaning beyond what the original author intended and beyond the literal meaning of the text. Let us envision individuals who, inspired by the fuller meaning, glean a surprising personal message from this difficult text and act on it. A deacon consults a biblical commentary to learn more about the Letter to the Hebrews, which he is addressing in his homily. A mother who finds comfort in her daily meditation on selected gospel passages enriches her prayer life by concluding her meditation with one of the psalms. A Catholic with a rather gloomy piety develops a more balanced spirituality by putting more emphasis on Christ's obedience than his sufferings. A hard-driving executive in the habit of imposing his will on people who work for him becomes more effective by respecting and listening to them. A young woman who takes for granted the many opportunities she enjoys in life learns a little history and comes to appreciate how women of previous generations suffered and struggled to open doors for women today. A man who regularly goes to Mass with his wife without actively participating surprises her at the Christmas Eve Mass by participating and even receiving communion.

What personal message can I find in this passage from Hebrews?

7. DOING GOOD DESPITE OUR LIMITATIONS

As we strive to live the gospel in our circle of influence despite our sins and weaknesses, we can find encouragement from the personal witness of the Apostle Paul found in 2 Corinthians 12:7–10: "That I [Paul] might not become too elevated [because of the abundance of the revelations], a thorn in the flesh was given to me, an angel of Satan, to beat me, to keep me from being too elated." Paul, who had a life-changing personal encounter with the risen Lord, among other deep spiritual experiences, recognized that these blessings could be a source of pride that would impede his ministry. Something in his life, however, has helped to keep him humble, a "thorn in the flesh" he calls it. It seems this weakness was perceptible to others and was embarrassing to Paul. Scripture scholars are not sure what it was, but many suggest some type of physical ailment or limitation. Paul asked the Lord to remove this weakness but received this response: "My grace is sufficient for you, for power is made perfect in weakness." The Apostle interprets this response positively. In fact, he will accept his sufferings and even boast of his weakness so that Christ's power can work through him, "for when I am weak, then I am strong."

We can use this passage to reflect on our own weaknesses and limitations from the perspective of the way God's power is at work in our lives. As graced beings threatened by sin, we are a mixture of strengths and weaknesses. It is possible to misread our limitations in two fundamental ways: to ignore them, thus impeding our spiritual growth, or to overemphasize them, restricting our efforts to do good. From a faith perspective, we can view our weaknesses more positively as a catalyst for growing in humility and developing greater reliance on God's power. As Paul understood, God can use us as instruments for spreading the kingdom despite our limitations. This faith conviction encourages us to trust God and do our best despite our limitations.

We probably all know stories of persons who exemplify the truth of the epistle. There are those who have effectively worked twelve-step programs based on their trust in a higher power and their realization that they are powerless over their addiction. There are the veterans, maimed in war, who, sustained by their faith, worked their way through long, demanding rehab programs and became once again productive citizens. I am recalling a collegian who wanted to be a lector at Mass but was not a very good reader. Given the opportunity, he spent time prayerfully reflecting on his assigned reading, so he better understood its meaning and practicing it out loud with his girlfriend. Over time, he became an effective proclaimer of the scriptures. A middle-aged executive, realizing his lack of self-control was leading him into an unhealthy romantic relationship with his secretary, prayed to God for forgiveness and strength. Following the advice of his pastor, he broke off the budding affair and concentrated on improving his relationship with his wife.

How has God used me to accomplish some good despite my limitations?

8. PRACTICING THE SIMPLE GOSPEL MESSAGE

All Christians are called to spread the faith, to share the good news, to proclaim the gospel. Most of us do this most effectively not by words but by deeds, not by public proclamation but by good example. The Apostle Paul knew this truth by experience. In 1 Corinthians, Paul comments on his approach to preaching the gospel in Corinth, a cosmopolitan seaport city. Before coming to Corinth, he preached in Athens, the symbolic center of Greek culture. In a cleverly crafted sermon, he noted that the "unknown God" they worshiped was really the Creator who made the whole world and gives to everyone "life and breath and everything" (Acts 17:23–25). This God will "judge the world with justice" through a man raised from the dead (17:31). At this, the cultured Athenians scoffed at him and dismissed him, saying they would hear him again on this matter some other time. Chastened by this failure to connect with the Athenians, Paul came to Corinth with a new approach.

As he puts it in 1 Corinthians, he proclaimed "the mystery of God," to you not with "sublimity of words" but by concentrating on "Jesus Christ, and him crucified." Paul goes on to admit that he came to the Corinthians in "weakness and fear and much trembling," not with "persuasive (words of) wisdom" but in the power of the Spirit, "so that your faith might rest not on human wisdom but on the power of God" (2:1–5).

In a culture that valued eloquent public speaking, Paul turned his own limitations as a preacher into the wise strategy of letting the power of the gospel speak for itself. Christ crucified and risen is himself the good news, the revelation of God's love, the source of salvation for all.

There are no single perfect messengers of Christ: not Paul, not the best of popes, not theologians, not homilists, not religion teachers, and not parents trying to instruct their children in the ways of the faith. But the whole people of God, anointed by the Spirit, has kept alive the memory of Christ and preserved his fundamental teaching. As individuals like Paul, Mother Teresa, and Pope Francis remind us, the gospel of Christ in its beauty and simplicity has an amazing power to touch our minds and hearts.

I can imagine various distinct responses to this epistle. A Christian feminist develops a more positive outlook on the Apostle Paul as a truly humble man. A conservative Catholic, upset with some progressive views of Pope Francis, decides he is going to stay in the Church he loves because he finds Christ there. A father of three realizes the best way to instruct his children is by living his faith. A woman who is generally disappointed in her pastor's homilies still tries to find some point she can use for further reflection.

How can I best share the good news of Jesus Christ?

9. EXPANDING OUR HORIZONS

As Christians, we all have a limited understanding of essential elements of our faith, such as God's plan of salvation. This means that we are called to an ongoing process of expanding and deepening our understanding of the faith. In this effort, Ephesians 1:3–14 provides us with a helpful broad overview of God's cosmic plan of salvation in Christ. The author praises God for many gifts freely given in and through Christ granting us "every spiritual blessing in the heavens"; choosing us "before the foundations of the world, to be holy and without blemish"; destining us "for adoption to himself"; redeeming us and forgiving our "transgressions"; and making known to us the divine plan "for the fullness of times, to sum up all things in Christ, in heaven and on earth." Put schematically, God has called us to holiness, made us adopted members of the divine family, redeemed us from sin, and revealed to us the great plan of salvation for all. This divine plan is clearly christocentric, emphasizing the role of Jesus Christ as our brother, exemplar, and savior, who reveals the power and extent of God's unconditional love for us. This epistle, with its grand poetic vision of salvation history,

encourages us to expand our horizons, to rejoice in our blessings, to imagine new possibilities, and to love more generously. We possess an intrinsic dignity as children of God that
is more important than any of our weaknesses. Our vocation
to holiness can be pursued in any state of life, any career,
and any job. Christian faith is more about committing ourselves to Christ than accepting doctrines and keeping rules.
The story of our everyday life, with its joys and sorrows, is
encompassed by a larger story that ends in the final victory
of good over evil.

We can imagine Christians responding to the epistle
in various positive ways. A man who grew up thinking only
Catholics can be saved could come to realize that faithful members of other religions are also children of God. A
grandmother who has great devotion to the Blessed Virgin
Mary could deepen her spirituality by gaining a better appreciation of the humanity of Jesus Christ our supreme model
and mediator. A shy young woman overly conscious of her
limitations could gain greater self-confidence by meditating
on gospel stories of Jesus, the friend of outcasts. A stockbro-
ker totally immersed in the narrow world of finance could
embrace a larger spiritual world that values loving relationships, cultural achievements, and social justice.

What step could I take to broaden my Christian horizons?

10. VIEWING CHRIST'S DEATH AS A GIFT TO US

Some Christians today are not comfortable with the
word *sacrifice* referring to Christ's death and our liturgical
celebration of it, seeing it as an outdated word that suggests
ancient animal sacrifices. To deal with this concern we need
to revisit the Letter to the Hebrews, addressed to Jewish

Christians well versed in the ritual practices of Israel, including the Day of Atonement when the high priest entered the sanctuary of the temple and sacrificed goats and calves for the sins of the people (Heb 9:11–28). The author wants to show that Christ is the mediator of a new covenant and has fulfilled the promises made to Israel. He is the new high priest, who entered the heavenly sanctuary "not made by hands" and offered a sacrifice, not the blood of animals, but his own blood, a once-for-all offering that cleanses our consciences and obtains "eternal redemption" for us.

In reflecting on this passage from Hebrews, it is helpful to keep certain cautions in mind. First, the historical Jesus was not a priest, let alone the high priest, nor a member of the priestly aristocracy; he was a layman from a small town in Galilee. The notion that we are saved by the sacrificial blood of Jesus is one of several explanations of salvation found in the New Testament; for example, that Christ reconciled us to God by his obedience. Historically, an emphasis on the bloody sacrifice of Jesus has led to a popular piety that sees God as a harsh judge who demands horrible sufferings as a payment for sin. Traditionally, the Church has extended sacrifice language to the Eucharist, officially using the term, "the sacrifice of the Mass." Again, at a popular level, some Catholics viewed the Mass as an unbloody repetition of the bloody sacrifice of Jesus on the cross, a faulty conception that influenced the questionable practice of the multiplication of private Masses. Furthermore, many people today are not comfortable with the thought of offering sacrifices to a demanding God.

With these cautions in mind, we could speak about Christ's saving action not as a sacrifice but as a gift. God gave a great gratuitous gift to the human race by sending his son to share our life. In turn, Christ offered a gift to his Father, a dedicated life of obedient loving service that brought him to death on the cross. This total self-emptying of Jesus opened him up for the gift of a permanent place at the right hand of his Father. In the eucharistic liturgy, we receive the gift of Christ's presence in the assembly, the scriptural word, and the sharing of the sacred meal. Grateful for our union with Christ, we respond by offering the gift of ourselves with all our daily efforts to love God and our neighbor as well as our good intentions to share in the mission of the risen Lord.

Perhaps some Catholics can benefit from reinterpreting Christ's sacrifice as a form of gift giving. Those charged with handing on the faith could explain salvation in ways more understandable to young persons. Those who come to Mass regularly merely as spectators could become more active participants. Those who see liturgy primarily as a way of fulfilling their obligation to worship the unseen God could come to recognize their responsibility to love the people they see in everyday life. Those who doubt their worthiness to receive communion could see it as a gift that no one deserves or merits.

How could reinterpreting Christ's sacrifice for me as a generous gift enrich my spiritual life?

11. FOSTERING A HEALTHY PLURALISM

As we deal with various forms of polarization in the Church, we can find guidance in 1 Corinthians 3:16–23. There Paul reminds the Corinthians that they are "the temple of God" and that "the Spirit of God" dwells in the community and all the members, making them holy. Paul had in mind the Jewish temple in Jerusalem, which imposed severe penalties on Gentiles entering its inner court where God dwelled. For Paul, the local community of faith established by Christ is now the new dwelling place of the Holy Spirit. Those disciples who threaten the unity of the Church will be subject to divine punishment, as Paul warns: "God will destroy that person."

Paul then repeats one of his favorite themes, the superiority of divine wisdom over worldly wisdom: "For the wisdom of this world is foolishness in the eyes of God." For the Corinthians, it is worldly foolishness for them to give their allegiance to a particular teacher, whether Paul, Apollos, or Cephas. The deeper truth provided by divine wisdom is that they belong to Christ and Christ belongs to God. As a temple of the Holy Spirit united to Christ, the Corinthian church has a responsibility to avoid division based on personalities and foster unity grounded in Christ.

Throughout history, Christians have had their favorite saints chosen among many great ones like Mary and Joseph, Monica and Augustine, Teresa of Avila and John of the Cross, Mother Teresa and Oscar Romero. Catholics have favorite popes, for example, some prefer John Paul II and others John XXIII. All this diversity has, for the most part, enriched the Christian church and not diminished it. The problem arises when a healthy pluralism devolves into a destructive polarization, as happened in Corinth. When polarization prevails, it stifles dialogue, demonizes opponents, and makes an idol out of partial truth.

Paul reminds us that the way beyond division is to unite on shared commitment to Christ. Our fundamental commandment is not to any saint or pope. We commit ourselves primarily to Jesus Christ, the Wisdom of the Father.

A conservative Catholic who reveres John Paul the Great became more open to dialogue with liberal Catholics when he began to hear the voice of Christ speaking through Pope Francis. A Vatican II Catholic gained greater appreciation for Pope Benedict XVI when she read his book *Jesus of Nazareth,* which highlights the centrality of Christ. Focusing on Christ brings us closer together.

What can I do to promote unity in my parish?

12. DEVELOPING A HEALTHY ATTITUDE TOWARD OUR BODIES

In 1 Corinthians 15:45–49, Paul encourages us to take seriously our fundamental Christian belief in the resurrection of the body—a crucial doctrine that rules out negative attitudes toward the human body.

The Apostle contrasts our earthly physical body that we have as offspring of the first man, Adam, with the heavenly body we will have by sharing in the risen life of the last Adam, Jesus Christ, by noting, "It is written, 'The first man, Adam, became a living being,' the last Adam a life-giving spirit." Adam received life from God; Christ, through his death and resurrection, shared his risen life with us. The short passage concludes, "Just as we have borne the image of the earthly one [Adam], we shall also bear the image of the heavenly one [Christ]."

By birth, we share in the common life of all the descendants of Adam and Eve. We know joys and sorrows, highs and lows, victories and defeats, successes and failures, celebrations and routines, growth and diminishments, delight and pain. Our common journey leads inevitably toward the final boundary of death.

By virtue of our baptism, we share in the death and resurrection of Christ. This does not lift us out of the human condition but invests the whole adventure with deeper meaning. Christ accompanies us on our journey, providing energy and enlightenment. We find wisdom in his teaching and inspiration in his exemplary life. We share in his mission to spread the reign of God in the world. The blessing of participating in the glorified life of Christ is a gift, not earned; a pure grace, not merited.

As we wend our way through life, we travel by faith, not by sight. We believe Christ walks with us, but his presence remains mysterious, often hidden, unavoidably partial and incomplete. It is possible with God's grace to deepen that relationship, to become more aware of the Lord's presence, to share more wholeheartedly in his mission. It is only in and through death, however, that we share completely in the risen life of Christ. Then, as Paul teaches us, our earthly body, inherited from the first Adam, will be transformed into a heavenly body informed by Christ, the second Adam. The Apostle, himself blessed by an appearance of the risen Lord, does not tell us what a resurrected human body is like, but he does assure us that we, as whole persons, will share in Christ's victory over death.

The epistle's positive outlook on the human body has an important message and encouraging word for people today dealing with a great variety of challenges: those looking for motivation to start and maintain a regular exercise program; those struggling with substance abuse problems; those attempting to improve their health by losing weight; those striving to gain a more mature attitude toward human sexuality; those seeking a reason to avoid pornography, which demeans women; those unhappy with their bodies; those seeking to accept gracefully the physical diminishments of age; and those praying for inner peace as they face the darkness of imminent death.

How can I benefit from a healthy Christian attitude toward the human body?

13. REFLECTING ON THE SIGNIFICANCE OF THE RESURRECTION

We can never exhaust the profound significance of the resurrection for our lives as Christians. The important fifteenth chapter of 1 Corinthians connects the resurrection of Christ with our own resurrection. Verses 12 through 20 deal with the question of the resurrection of the dead. Evidently, there were Christian converts in Corinth who in one way or another denied the resurrection of the body. In response, Paul writes, "If Christ is preached as raised from the dead, how can some of you say there is no resurrection of the dead?" Throughout his defense of the resurrection, Paul assumes the intimate connection between Christ and his followers. "If the dead are not raised, neither has Christ been raised," then our faith is vain, and we are still in our sins. Furthermore, if Christ was not raised, then those who died have perished and those who have hoped in Christ for this life only are "the most pitiable people of all." Paul concludes the passage: "But now Christ has been raised from the dead, the firstfruits of those who have fallen asleep."

Paul's positive conclusion invites further reflection on the meaning of the resurrection. The God who sent Christ into the world and raised him to life is totally trustworthy and completely faithful to the divine promises. The resurrection vindicates the claims of Jesus to be the absolute savior and definitive prophet. It means grace is more powerful than sin and that love is stronger than all the dark forces, including death. By baptism, we share in the death and resurrection of Christ. As we journey through life we are strengthened and guided by the Holy Spirit, the Advocate bestowed on us through the intercession of Christ. When we move through the passageway of death, we continue to share in the life of the risen Christ. We give expression to this truth by affirming both the resurrection of the body and the immortality of the soul, which indicates that we, as whole integrated persons, are destined for everlasting happiness in heaven with Christ. Belief in the resurrected Christ means we trust that our sins are forgiven, that our deceased loved ones are with God, and that we will one day join them in the everlasting kingdom, where our deepest longings are fulfilled and our tears are wiped away.

The epistle, which prompts reflection on the meaning of the resurrection, provides good news for us today. For those walking in the dark valley of dejection and doubt, the resurrection proclaims that the human journey is meaningful and has a fulfilling goal. For those anxious about dying, it provides comfort by teaching that death is a passageway to eternal life. For those grieving the loss of loved ones, it gives assurance that they now live with God, in everlasting happiness. Finally, for those struggling with guilt feelings, resurrection faith reminds us that Christ died and rose to make expiation for our sins.

What aspect of resurrection faith can help me to grow spiritually?

14. APPLYING DIVINE WISDOM TO MORAL ISSUES

As we look for guidance in living the Christian life in our secular world, let us reflect on 1 Corinthians 2:6–10, where the Apostle Paul instructs on true wisdom. When Paul was writing in the middle 50s, a worldview common among both Jews and Gentiles contrasted "this age" of waiting with "the age to come," when the secrets of the universe would be revealed. Paul reminds the Corinthians that he did not speak to them with a wisdom of this age, a worldly wisdom of the rulers who put Jesus to death. Rather, he treated them as "mature" persons, proclaiming "God's wisdom, mysterious, hidden, which God predetermined before the ages for our glory." Quoting an unknown author, Paul writes, "What eye has not seen, and ear has not heard, and what has not entered the human heart," suggesting the ultimately mysterious character of the divine plan of salvation. However, through the Spirit, who "scrutinizes everything, even the depths of God," we know something of what God has in store for us.

Paul encourages us to reflect on ways that divine wisdom challenges worldly wisdom today. Our culture, for example, suggests that having more things is the way to achieve happiness. Divine wisdom teaches us that being is more important than having, that acquiring more possessions does not satisfy the deepest longings of the heart, that spiritual growth is more fulfilling than financial gain. An affluent executive found greater inner peace when she simplified her lifestyle by giving away some of her prized wardrobe, limiting her new purchases, and increasing her charitable contributions.

In our society today there is a worldly wisdom with some questionable assumptions about sex: it is an autonomous possession available to maximize pleasure; the more sex the better; sexual restraint makes no sense; guilt over sex is neurotic. There is a Christian outlook on sex inspired by divine wisdom: sex is a gift from God to be used responsibly; physical expression should reflect commitment; a faithful permanent marriage provides the best setting for spouses to grow together in various dimensions of their lives, physically, emotionally, morally, intellectually, and spiritually. A husband celebrating ten years of a happy, fulfilling marriage is grateful to God for rescuing him from the promiscuous lifestyle of his collegiate years, which left him feeling empty, and calling him to marriage, which demanded fidelity.

What specific step could I take to incorporate divine wisdom in my own life?

15. DISCERNING THE BEST COURSE OF ACTION

Not all of our morally significant decisions are clearly covered by biblical wisdom, Church teaching, or general principles. There are situations where we must discern the most fitting thing to do by listening to the Holy Spirit and considering the good of others. In this regard, consider the way the Apostle Paul deals with whether Christians should eat food that was offered in idol worship (see 1 Cor 10:31—11:1). In general, Paul tells the Corinthians that they are free to eat whatever is sold in the market. Circumstances, however, could limit this freedom. For example, if someone calls attention to the fact that this food was used in idol worship, it is better not to eat it to avoid scandalizing others.

In this passage, Paul explains his advice: "Whether you eat or drink, or whatever you do, do everything for the glory of God. Avoid giving offense." In making decisions about food, the Corinthians should maintain a faith perspective, trying to do the Lord's will and promoting God's glory. Furthermore, they should be careful not to cause others to have doubts or fall into sin. Paul goes on to say he tries "to please everyone in every way, not seeking my own benefit but that of the many that they may be saved." In other words, do not give scandal to others, but positively promote their well-being. The Apostle concludes by advising the Corinthians to follow his example: "Be imitators of me, as I am of Christ."

Although we are no longer faced with the problem of eating food sacrificed to idols, we do exercise our freedom in communal contexts that affect other people. It is true that Christ freed us from legalistic concerns about slavishly following human rules. However, our actual exercise of Christian freedom makes an impact on other persons. Not everything that is legal is morally right. Not everything that is moral is proper or prudent. In discerning the most fitting course of action in any situation, we should prayerfully consider the promptings of the Holy Spirit as well as our obligation to avoid harming others and to promote their good.

Some composite examples can clarify Paul's teaching. A married woman voluntarily gives up a healthy innocent friendship with a male work colleague because it bothers her husband and hurts their marriage. A dedicated parishioner relinquishes his position as chair of the social justice committee so that younger persons have an opportunity to develop their leadership skills and make their contribution to the parish. A woman with a promising career refuses a promotion to preserve enough time for her children.

What legitimate thing should I voluntarily give up to avoid scandalizing others and to promote their well-being?

16. JUSTIFYING OUR HOPE

There are many good reasons for being discouraged about current developments in our country and our Church. In this situation we must count Christian hope as a great blessing that keeps us from giving up even when it is difficult to be optimistic. Given this gift, we do well to reflect on 1 Peter 3:15–18. It was probably written by a disciple of Peter, the first pope, sometime after his martyrdom in Rome during the persecution of Nero from 64 to 68. The letter was most likely addressed to Christian communities in northern Asia Minor (modern Turkey). Our passage repeats a common theme in the letter: bearing the sufferings that Christians endure for living their faith in a hostile environment. The author advises Christians to reverence Christ as "Lord in your hearts." Christ himself, the righteous one, suffered for our sins, "put to death in the flesh, he was brought to life in the spirit," that he might lead us to God.

The author reminds us as Christians, "Always be ready to give an explanation to anyone who asks you for a reason for your hope." We should do this with "gentleness and reverence," keeping our "conscience clear" so that those who malign and defame us will themselves "be put to shame."

Amid suffering, we are well advised to turn to Christ dwelling in our hearts, who saved us from our sins by his death and resurrection. We have a responsibility to explain the hope Christ inspires in us to anyone interested.

Let us imagine ordinary individuals giving effective witness to their Christian hope. Over the years, a father picked key moments to share with his growing son the ways his Christian faith helped him manage some of the crosses of life, like the death of his mother and a demotion at work. A wife talked her husband into doing a Marriage Encounter by emphasizing her hope that their marriage could be more mutually enriching. A grandmother comforts her collegiate granddaughter, who remains upset that the glass ceiling is still intact, by sharing her own experience of women's progress as a sign of hope for the future. A geology professor long worried about apathy over global warming found new hope when he saw the positive response of his students to the encyclical *Laudato Si'* by Pope Francis.

Am I prepared to explain the hope that sustains me in these challenging times?

17. BROADENING OUR PERSPECTIVE

In trying to maintain and justify the Vatican II teaching on salvation optimism, we do well to reflect on Ephesians 3:2–6. Ephesians, probably written by a disciple of Paul after his death sometime between AD 65 and 67, emphasizes the worldwide mission of the Church to bring salvation to all people. Drawing on the authority of Paul, who received "the stewardship of God's grace" made known to him by divine revelation, the author insists that "the Gentiles are coheirs, members of the same body, and copartners in the promise in Christ Jesus through the gospel." The vexing issue for the early Church was what to do about Gentile converts. Did they have to accept distinctive Jewish practices such as circumcision? Paul was the great advocate for welcoming Gentiles into the community of faith without religious preconditions. His viewpoint prevailed at the Council of Jerusalem around AD 49, setting the stage for the Jesus movement to spread throughout the world.

The Second Vatican Council unleashed a new spirit of inclusion by speaking positively of the world religions as vehicles of truth and goodness and by encouraging interfaith dialogue and cooperation. It endorsed a salvation optimism by teaching that even those who have not yet learned to call God by name can be saved if they follow their properly formed conscience.

Reflecting on Ephesians could challenge Christians today to rethink their more restrictive viewpoints. Those who think of Jews as God-killers could come to see them as fellow believers in the God of the Bible. Those who think of Buddhists as pagans could come to appreciate their rich traditions of meditation and compassion. Those who fear all Muslims as potential terrorists could come to view them as fellow monotheists and members of the Abrahamic family. Those who believe that atheistic humanists are sinners worthy of damnation could find ways to cooperate with them to serve the common good.

Do I harbor any exclusive attitudes that should be challenged?

18. LEARNING TO BE MORE INCLUSIVE

There seems to be a tribal instinct that moves us to gather with like-minded persons. Problems arise when this natural tendency leads to xenophobia, prejudice, and exclusionary practices. Over time, the Church has gradually come to realize the implications of the inclusive practice and teaching of Jesus.

In the first century of the Christian era, the community of believers wrestled with the question of how the Gentiles fit into God's plan of salvation. Jesus himself was a Jew who practiced the Jewish faith and, for the most part, confined his mission to the Jewish community. He did instruct his followers to preach the gospel to all nations, and by the middle of the first century the apostolic leaders reached agreement that Gentiles could join the Jesus movement without following all the Jewish laws and practices. Nevertheless, tensions over this issue remained late into the first century, as suggested by the Letter to the Ephesians, which emphasizes that God's plan of salvation is inclusive, embracing Jews and Gentiles. No one is excluded from the universal love of God.

Throughout history, Christians have known the temptation to exclude others, those who are different, from God's salvific plan, even Jewish and Muslim monotheists. In various documents, the Second Vatican Council (1962–65) rejected all prejudice and bigotry, while recognizing the world's religions as vehicles of truth and goodness and promoting interfaith dialogue and cooperation.

The inclusivism suggested by Ephesians and taught by Vatican II challenges all of us to overcome all xenophobic tendencies. We can think of persons who have done that. A man with strong anti-Semitic prejudice inherited from his family became friends with a Jewish colleague at work and now sees Jewish people as children of God and coheirs of heaven. A woman who assumed Islam was a religion of violence read more about it and now sees most Muslims as allies in the war against terrorism. A father who initially rejected his gay son prayed regularly for him and over time gradually softened his negative attitude, eventually leading to a tearful and loving reconciliation with him. A white employer with hidden racist tendencies was so impressed by the great job performance of her black employees that she recognized her prejudice and consciously rejected it. A generally open-minded Republican father was secretly upset that his daughter married a leftist Democrat but over time came to like his son-in-law, recognizing in the process the danger of demonizing political opponents.

What are my own exclusive blind spots?

19. PROMOTING CHRISTIAN INCLUSIVISM

Unfortunately, today we are experiencing in the United States a rise of xenophobia, a fear or hatred of those who are foreigners, strangers, or "other" in some way. In promoting a more inclusive Christian response, we can learn some important lessons from the Letter to the Ephesians, which makes it clear that salvation is available to all, not through the bloodline of Abraham, but through membership in the

Body of Christ, not through following the Jewish law, but through commitment to Christ and his law of love. God calls all people to be copartners in the mission of Christ to spread the reign of God in the world. All the things that divide us are less important than being coheirs, comembers, and copartners in and through Christ.

Historically, that crucial insight enabled the Jesus movement, begun by a Jewish messiah and led by his Jewish disciples, to become a transnational world religion, an inclusive community of believers, a Christian faith tradition capable of informing and transforming all cultures in every historical period.

Today, the universalism of Ephesians challenges the restrictions imposed by new forms of tribalism. Especially troubling are the strains of American nationalism that foster fear and resentment of those who are "other": non-Christians, racial minorities, refugees, immigrants, foreigners, gay persons, feminists, and any other group that is different enough to be perceived as a threat. From a Christian perspective, such exclusivity is morally wrong because it violates Christ's command to love our neighbor, especially the most vulnerable, and undercuts his mission to establish an inclusive community of love. Furthermore, exclusive nationalism disregards our country's highest ideals of welcoming refugees and immigrants, celebrating diversity, and ensuring God-given human rights for all.

As Christians, we have a moral responsibility to do all we can, depending on our situation, to help our country live up to its promise of inclusion. Elected representatives can build bipartisan coalitions to pass legislation that makes our society more inclusive. Teachers can help their students appreciate past struggles for equal justice, including voting rights for women and blacks. Grandparents can tell their grandchildren the stories of their ancestors who first came to this country, reminding them that we are all offspring of immigrants. White parents can welcome into their homes black and brown friends of their children. We can all speak positively of those who are different and challenge all forms of discrimination and prejudice.

What is the most important thing I can do to promote Christian inclusivism?

20. DEVELOPING A MORE BALANCED SPIRITUALITY

The current American interest in spirituality is a positive trend but can easily give way to fads and superficial approaches. We need a solid theology to guide our spiritual quest in healthy directions. The First Letter of Peter offers some important theological themes to guide our quest. In general, the letter highlights the blessings we enjoy because of the death and resurrection of Christ. The author prefers long complex Greek sentences (it's hard to believe that a Galilean fisherman who spoke Aramaic wrote them) that makes it difficult to follow his line of argument.

The relevant passage (1:17–21) reminds those of us who invoke God as Father, our merciful judge, to "conduct [ourselves] with reverence" during our "sojourn," presumably our journey to heaven, realizing that we were ransomed, or bought back, not by gold or silver but by the blood of Christ, the "spotless unblemished lamb," reminiscent of the Jewish Passover meal. Christ's presence in human history, "known before the foundation of the world" enables us to put our "faith and hope" in God, who raised Jesus from the dead and "gave him glory."

We can detect several theological themes in this passage that can help us develop a balanced spirituality: God is like a father who is head of a household; we are on a journey leading to eternal happiness with God; Christ, with God from all eternity, redeemed us by his death and resurrection; salvation is available for us now but will be complete only at the end-time; we should live reverently, not following the futile standards of the world, but acting according to who we really are, children of God redeemed by Christ.

Christians who engage with this reading could develop a more balanced spiritual life. A collegian with a limited image of God as a doting father could remember that God is also the judge who expects her to live as a responsible adult. A retired executive drifting through life could come to see himself on a meaningful journey toward greater personal authenticity and the ultimate fulfillment of his deepest longings. An engineer who links her self-worth with having expensive things could shift her emphasis to becoming a better person, wife, mother, friend, and colleague. A nurse who feels underappreciated could develop a deeper faith that he is indeed doing God's work in the world. A mechanic who regularly attends Sunday Mass mostly out of habit could have a more fruitful encounter with the risen Lord by participating actively and consciously in the liturgy.

How can theology help me develop a more balanced spirituality?

21. FACING OUR SINFULNESS

In our culture we are reluctant to talk about sin in social settings and even in church. The author of 1 John dealt directly with this problem in 2:1–5: "My children, I am writing this to you so that you may not commit sin." The author, representing the authentic tradition of the community of the Beloved Disciple, presents himself as a wise teacher imparting practical wisdom to students tempted to ignore the reality of sin. Toward the end of the first century, some dissidents in the community claimed that those with a special knowledge of Jesus were saved and did not have to worry about committing sins or keeping the commandments. Today there are other reasons to avoid talking about sin: it carries too many negative connotations; it is easier and more productive to talk about neuroses; it produces unwarranted guilt feelings; it underplays God's mercy; it distorts the joy of the gospel.

This epistle encourages us to face the reality of sin because Jesus Christ, our "Advocate with the Father," is "expiation" for our sins and for the sins of the whole world. We can admit our sinfulness because Christ, the righteous one, has atoned for our sins and intercedes before God on our behalf.

The author of the epistle insists on the fundamental connection between a real personal knowledge of Christ and keeping his commandment to love God and neighbor. Those who say they know Christ but do not keep his commandments are "liar[s], and the truth is not in [them]."

The epistle reminds us that sin threatens all of us and pervades the entire world. We can face this reality because Christ has definitively ensured the final triumph of grace over all forms of sin and evil. Our faith in Christ should lead us to do our best to follow the Lord's command to love God and neighbor. There is a fundamental deceit in calling ourselves Christians but failing to follow his teaching.

We can imagine Christians responding positively to the epistle. Preachers and teachers who almost never talk about sin because they are uncomfortable with its heavy moralistic overtones, could reintroduce the word, explaining it in more acceptable terms, such as a failure to love or giving up on the goal of coming closer to Christ. Men who have been in the habit of demeaning women, whether overtly or subtly, could recognize that this is a sinful violation of the law of love and begin to treat women with greater respect. Believers who regularly examine their conscience according to the Ten Commandments could also assess their behavior according to the high ideals of Christ's law of love.

How could I face my sinfulness with greater honesty and deeper trust in Christ?

22. UNDERSTANDING JUSTIFICATION BY FAITH

In the sixteenth century, the Protestant Reformation spawned a long-standing debate between Catholics and Protestants on the nature of justification, with both sides holding firm to their fundamental position. Today, Catholic and Protestant scholars and leaders have come to a common agreement that we are saved by faith in God's grace, which prompts us to do good works. Now each side can learn from the other; for example, Catholics can look more deeply at Paul's classic statement in Romans 5:1–8. The Apostle begins with his fundamental conviction that we are justified by faith and goes on to explain what this means and how it was accomplished. To be justified means that we are in a right relationship with God, that we are at peace with our Creator, that we share in divine righteousness, and that we can "boast in hope of the glory of God." We are justified, not because of our own merits, but because Christ died for us "at the appointed time," while we were still sinners. This proves God's love for us, which "has been poured out into our hearts through the holy Spirit that has been given to us." Paul insists that Christian hope "does not disappoint" because God's grace is given to us so abundantly, poured into our hearts like water that gives life and refreshment.

Our hope for the ultimate fulfillment of our deepest

longings is based not on our own efforts or achievements but on God's overflowing love for us manifested by Christ's death and resurrection and communicated by the Holy Spirit poured into our hearts. Christ has won salvation for us, and the Holy Spirit resides within us. For our part, we must cooperate with God's grace by putting on the mind of Christ and responding to the promptings of the Spirit. As justified believers we now share in the righteousness of God, which promotes human flourishing and promises eternal life.

Let us imagine individuals who have grown spiritually by reflecting on this passage from Romans. An elderly man who spends long hours at night worrying about the salvation of his soul develops greater trust in a God who loves him despite his sins, which leads to more restful nights. A surgeon meditates for weeks on the image of the Holy Spirit poured into her heart and gradually becomes more attentive to gentle nudges from the Spirit throughout her day, including the hours in the operating room. By reading the passage carefully a couple of times, a committed Catholic gains a better understanding of the Protestant position on justification by faith alone. A waitress struck by the all-inclusive character of justification resolves to treat all her customers with respect, even those who don't deserve it.

Which part of Paul's treatment of justification most speaks to my heart?

23. LIVING OUR BAPTISMAL VOCATION

The Second Vatican Council generated renewed emphasis on the sacrament of baptism as our initiation into the Church and our sharing in the death and resurrection of Christ. The council made clear that by virtue of our baptism we all are equal members of the Church called to a life of holiness and service to the kingdom. Many Catholics are still trying to appropriate this teaching. In Romans 6:3–11, Paul expands our understanding of Christian baptism. In the early Church, candidates stepped down into the font, were immersed in the water, and came out the other side, where they received new white garments and a lit candle. The ritual signifies and actualizes our dying with Christ and partaking in his risen life. Thus, Paul writes, "Are you unaware that we who were baptized into Christ Jesus were baptized into his death?" Christ who died to sin once and for all dies no more. He has been raised to "newness of life" by the "glory of the Father." By baptism we share in the risen life of Christ. Paul assures us, "If, then, we have died with Christ, we believe that we shall also live with him." We live for Christ as he "lives for God." The passage concludes with an admonition: "Consequently, you too must think of yourselves as [being] dead to sin and living for God in Christ Jesus." Our baptism calls us to holiness, an ongoing process of dying to sin and living a life of fidelity to Christ, who taught us, "Whoever finds his life will lose it, and whoever loses his life for my sake will find it" (Matt 10:39). Following Christ demands dying to selfishness and living the law of love that brings new life.

We can imagine examples of individuals who have died to sin and are living the new life of Christ. An elderly husband who through his whole marriage has selfishly considered his own interests and needs more important than his wife's does a complete turnaround when she gets sick and gives himself to caring for her. A collegian who has spent his first three years doing more partying than studying gets his priorities straight for his senior year, improves his grades, and is accepted into grad school. A woman who works in the sex trade to support her heroin addiction admits herself into a rehab program, kicks her drug habit, gets a decent job, and starts a new life.

What concrete step could I take to die to sin and share more fully in the risen life of Christ?

24. CONTRIBUTING TO CHARITIES

As Christians we have a moral responsibility to manage our finances generously and wisely. It is instructive to recall how the Apostle Paul met that responsibility amid his ministry to the Gentiles. As a provision of the agreement reached at the Council of Jerusalem in 49, which welcomed uncircumcised Gentiles into the Christian community, Paul rededicated himself to raising money to support the beleaguered Jerusalem church. Second Corinthians 8:1–15 contains Paul's pitch to the Christians in Corinth to contribute generously to the Jerusalem collection. He made his case in three main points. The Corinthians had already received an abundance of spiritual gifts, and so it would be fitting for them to contribute generously to help others. His next point is theological, although expressed in economic terms: "For you know the gracious act of our Lord Jesus Christ, that for your sake he became poor although he was rich, so that by his poverty you might become rich." In other words, since the Son of God, one with his Father from all eternity, gave us the extremely generous gift of becoming man and sharing the limitations of the human condition, we should be generous in sharing our gifts with others. Finally, Paul made it clear that he is not asking the Corinthians to impoverish themselves but to share their financial abundance with the Jerusalem Christians, who have shared their spiritual gifts with Gentile converts. The passage ends with an obscure quote from Exodus: "Whoever had much did not have more, and whoever had little did not have less," referring to God's generous gift of manna in the desert to the Israelites that satisfied everyone's need. The point seems to be that God blesses all of us with gifts according to our needs.

The epistle reminds us that the Christian community has always been involved in the practical necessity of fundraising. It also teaches us to share our resources wisely and generously, because God has blessed us abundantly, especially by sending Christ as our Savior.

We can imagine examples of individuals who have appropriated that message. A single mother working two part-time jobs to support herself and her daughter thoughtfully budgets a set amount of money each week to put in the collection at Sunday Mass. A well-off man who thought he contributed generously to charities discovers he has been donating only about 1 percent of his income, leading him to double his contribution. A family spends some time investigating which of the many charitable requests they receive are most worthy of support. A widow who has inherited a large amount of money works hard and wisely to maximize its effective use: studying what others similarly blessed have done, hiring a lawyer trained in philanthropy, setting up a foundation with a dedicated board of advisers, employing the best financial investor available, and establishing grant proposal guidelines that privileged groups already efficiently assisting the needy.

How could I share my financial resources more generously and prudently?

25. LIVING IN THE PRESENT

Our attitude toward the future influences the way we live in the present. That dynamic relationship between present and future is addressed in 2 Thessalonians 2:1–17, which raises the issue of the second coming of Christ. The author warns his readers "not to be shaken out of your minds suddenly, or to be alarmed" by any indication, whether delivered orally or by letter, "to the effect that the day of the Lord is at hand."

There was an expectation in the early Church that Christ would return soon to complete his saving work. The Apostle Paul taught that the death and resurrection of Christ inaugurated a new age, and that the end-time had already arrived and would be completed when Christ returns. In 2 Thessalonians this final saving event is identified by the Greek word *Parousia*, which in the ancient Greek world referred to the solemn arrival of a king or emperor and is still commonly used today in Christian theology to refer to the ultimate completion of Christ's salvific work.

This teaching was intended to give the early Christians hope, especially as they endured hardships and disappointments. It encouraged them to stay awake and be alert, since the Parousia was coming soon and could come suddenly. Unfortunately, this teaching was at times misinterpreted, motivating some Christians to quit their jobs, not get married, and drop out of society. Some believers saw Christ's return in relation to the Jewish "day of the Lord," which carried connotations of judgment generating more fear than hope. Such misunderstandings probably generated the strong warning in the verse about not being shaken out of your minds.

Although most Christians today do not have an active expectation of an imminent Parousia, this epistle can still prompt a fruitful reflection on our attitude toward the future. Today we live between two decisive events: the paschal mystery of Christ and the final fulfillment of God's saving plan. For us, God's reign is already here but not yet complete, which alerts us to signs of progress toward greater justice and peace in our troubled world. Personally, we all face the inevitable boundary of death. Our days are shadowed by death as we make our pilgrim way on earth. By the decisions we make daily, we are making ourselves to be who we will be forever. Although the future remains for us dark, essentially unknowable, our faith tells us that death is a passageway to a new richer life with Christ, to the eternal bliss of heaven where our deepest longings are fulfilled and there are no more tears.

These faith convictions about the future can help us live more productive lives in the present. Those sleepwalking through life could wake up to the divine call to live life fully. Those excessively anxious about a final judgment could learn to trust God's mercy. Those overwhelmed by the evil in the world could look for positive developments in the daily news. Those sitting on the sidelines of life could start to meet their responsibilities to spread God's reign in their own circle of influence. We could all grow spiritually by developing a healthier attitude toward the future.

How does Christian teaching on the future help me live more fully in the present?

26. TRUSTING THAT OUR DECEASED LOVED ONES ARE WITH GOD

As we ponder the fate of our deceased loved ones, we can find hope in 1 Thessalonians 4:13–18. When Paul wrote this letter to the Church in Thessalonica, Greece, in AD 51, he and his converts commonly believed that the Lord Jesus, crucified and risen, would return soon to complete his work of definitively establishing God's reign, probably in their own lifetime. But they were worried about the fate of their loved ones who had already died before the Lord's return.

So that his beloved converts "may not grieve like the

rest, who have no hope," Paul assures them that their fundamental belief "that Jesus died and rose" means that God will
join their deceased loved ones with the Lord in his victory over
death. Basing his teaching "on the word of the Lord," Paul
insists that when Christ returns, he will first raise the dead
and then gather the living to himself, so that all the believers
will be with the Lord forever. To make his point, the Apostle
employs traditional Jewish apocalyptic language to describe
Christ's Parousia or second coming: "For the Lord himself,
with a word of command, with the voice of an archangel and
with the trumpet of God, will come down from heaven, and
the dead in Christ will rise first. Then we who are alive, who
are left, will be caught up together with them in the clouds
to meet the Lord in the air." Once again responding to the
initial worry of the Thessalonians, Paul concludes, "Console
one another with these words."

Today, Christians who no longer worry about the imminent return of Christ still find consolation in the faith conviction that our loved ones who died are with the Lord, sharing
in his victory over death and in his glorified risen life. A
widow after forty-nine years of a good marriage enjoys great
comfort in an abiding sense that her husband is still present
to her in ways that defy words. A philosophy professor who
has serious intellectual doubts about an afterlife finds that
he can best handle the premature death of his oldest son by
simply assuming he is somehow in a better place. A collegian periodically talks to her deceased father about her deepest joys and sorrows, convinced that he cares and listens. A
husband who is depressed after the death of his wife from
brain cancer can sometimes find relief by concentrating on
his faith conviction that she is with God and suffers no more.

How do I handle the deaths of my closest loved ones?

27. CELEBRATING THE MASS AS A GIFT EXCHANGE

The Second Vatican Council taught us that the Eucharist is the font and summit of the Christian life. Catholic spirituality is always interested in how we can enrich our celebration of the eucharistic liturgy. A section in Hebrews (10:11–18) could spark further reflection on the nature and meaning of the eucharistic liturgy. In this passage, the unknown but articulate author begins by noting the limitations of the Jewish priests who offered frequent sacrifices that "can never take away sins." The author then points out that Christ, our priest, "offered one sacrifice for sins" that "has made perfect forever those who are being consecrated." Having reconciled all of us with God, he took his seat forever at the right hand of God, where he intercedes for us and "waits until his enemies are made his footstool." Since our priest has accomplished the forgiveness of sins by his once-for-all sacrificial death on the cross, there is no longer a need for repeated sacrifices for sin.

The once-for-all sacrifice of Christ on the cross is a consistent theme in the Letter to the Hebrews. It reminds us that the eucharistic liturgy does not "repeat" the sacrifice of Christ on the cross. The *Catechism of the Catholic Church* explains that the Mass "re-presents" Christ's "once for all" self-sacrifice for us. The Eucharist is not a repetition of Calvary, but it is a memorial that makes present for us Christ's unique, once-for-all act of self-sacrificing love. Remembering Christ's death and resurrection at Mass makes the paschal mystery sacramentally present so we can share in it and draw on its saving power.

This understanding of the Mass can be enhanced by substituting the language of "gift giving" for the language of "offering sacrifice," which many see as obsolete because it suggests placating God by killing animals. We can say Christ offered the gift of himself, the gift of dedicated service, and the gift of his very life on the cross. In turn, he received the gift of risen life from the Father. When we participate in the liturgy, we can offer our gift of love and service to God in union with the risen Christ. The gifts of bread and wine brought to the altar can represent the gift of our lives, our joys and sorrows, our leisure and toil, our special moments and daily routine. Our gift of self is made holy by being joined to Christ, who is present in the assembly, the proclaimed word, and the consecrated bread and wine. Our full, active, conscious participation in the liturgy is our gift to God, mediated by Christ our high priest.

Reflecting on the Mass as a gift exchange that re-presents Christ's definitive act of self-giving love can enrich our participation in the eucharistic liturgy. A farmer who works long hours to support his family can see the bread brought to the altar as representing his efforts to put bread on the table. An elderly mother no longer needed by her independent son can feel useful by offering Sunday Mass for his intention. A happily married man with a wonderful family can express his gratitude to God by participating wholeheartedly in the liturgy. A mother fighting depression can continue to attend Mass, asking for God's help to keep meeting her responsibilities. A collegian blessed with a good singing voice can share his gift by singing in the parish choir.

How can I participate more fruitfully in the eucharistic gift exchange?

28. FINDING GREATER MEANING IN OUR WORK

Those of us interested in developing a deeper spirituality of work can consider a passage from 2 Thessalonians 3:6–16, where Paul tells the Christian community in Thessalonica to imitate him, especially the way he ministered among them, preaching the gospel but also working hard so as not to be a financial burden on them. He says he did not accept free food from anyone, but, on the contrary, he worked "in toil and drudgery, night and day" so as "not to burden any of you." As a preacher of the gospel, he had a "right" to compensation but did not exercise it so as to present himself as "a model" that they could imitate.

Paul goes on to admonish those who were not working; they might have thought the return of Christ was imminent or that they were too spiritual for such mundane tasks. He repeats a previous instruction that "if anyone was unwilling to work, neither should that one eat," instructing those who "are not keeping busy but minding the business of others" to "work quietly and to eat their own food."

We can use this passage as a springboard to further reflection on a contemporary spirituality of work. Work should not be equated with a job, as is often done today. Work includes all purposeful, meaningful activity that produces results and contributes to the common good. Mothers who spend untold hours caring for children and creating a home perform some of the most important work, although they are not paid for it. Work enables us to develop our talents and to know the satisfaction of accomplishment and contribution. Work is the way people earn a living, support themselves and their families. Some work is toil (burdensome, boring, unfulfilling, backbreaking) but must be done to survive and meet responsibilities to others.

Through our work, we share in God's ongoing creation of the world and help move the evolutionary process forward. All legitimate work is an extension of God's creative power and has an inherent dignity and worth. By working honestly and diligently, we build up the Body of Christ and spread the kingdom in the world.

We can imagine individuals who exemplify this contemporary spirituality of work. A checkout clerk in a grocery store who cannot find another job manages her boring job by trying to engage each customer in a positive way, for instance, remembering a name, listening attentively, saying a kind word, sharing a smile, and being extra helpful. The head of an advertising agency, who has built up the company, achieves greater productivity by treating each employee as a unique individual with specific talents and emotional needs. A first-grade teacher who prays for her students in the morning maintains a positive attitude by concentrating on preparing her students to be lifelong learners. A college basketball coach who recognizes his community responsibilities puts a lot of extra effort into helping his players succeed not only on the court but in the classroom as preparation for productive lives.

What aspect of a spirituality of work will help me?

29. TRANSFORMING AFFLICTIONS

As we contend with the inevitable afflictions of life, we can find a surprising suggestion in Romans 5:1–5. Paul begins by reminding us that "we have been justified by faith" and "have peace with God through our Lord Jesus Christ," and he includes the affirmation that "the love of God has been poured out into our hearts through the holy Spirit that has been given to us." He does not give us a developed doctrine of God, but he does suggest that the one God relates to us in three different ways as the Source of love and peace that we call the Father, as the Lord Jesus Christ who gives us access to the Father, and as the Holy Spirit who dwells in our hearts.

Paul insists that belief in the God who sent the Son and the Spirit for our salvation helps us manage the afflictions of everyday life. He writes, "We even boast of our afflictions, knowing that affliction produces endurance, and endurance, proven character, and proven character, hope, and hope does not disappoint."

We all know something of the afflictions built into human existence: moral failures, personal limitations, social constraints, physical suffering, emotional disturbances, family conflicts, broken friendships, and the distinctive crosses that we bear alone. Those afflictions can generate negative responses, draining our energy, upsetting our psychic equilibrium, depressing our spirit, distorting our thinking, hardening our heart, and weakening our faith.

Paul, however, wants us to boast of our afflictions, to transform them into catalysts for spiritual growth, so that we practice endurance, develop greater maturity, and maintain hope. Christian hope is based on fundamental faith convictions: that Christ has already given us access to the Father; that the Holy Spirit even now guides and strengthens us on our earthly journey; and that, one day, Christ will complete his mission by defeating all the dark forces, and the Holy Spirit will transform all afflictions so that God's peace and love will reign supreme.

It is possible for individuals to practice the virtue of hope anonymously without explicit reference to the triune God, as the salvation optimism taught by Vatican II suggests. As Christians, however, we believe that trinitarian faith can help us develop and practice the virtue of hope that transforms afflictions into virtuous action.

We have heard stories of persons who exemplify this process. Mothers afflicted by the tragedy of losing their children in car accidents involving alcohol who formed the advocacy group known as MADD (Mothers Against Drunk

Driving). Persons afflicted with the disease of alcoholism who joined AA (Alcoholics Anonymous) remained sober for years and now serve as sponsors for others doing the twelve-step program. Veterans afflicted with serious wounds in battle who came home, rehabilitated, and volunteered to help other veterans with emotional problems. Wealthy prominent athletes afflicted by an early life of poverty who established programs to help disadvantaged youth. Survivors afflicted by clergy sex abuse who found ways to help other victims and call perpetrators to account.

What specific step could I take to transform one of my afflictions?

30. AVOIDING COMPLACENCY

On our spiritual journey we may be tempted to slack off, to rest on our laurels, to be satisfied with our limited progress, to grow weary of our effort to be more faithful disciples of Christ. A proper interpretation of Hebrews 4:12–13 can help us surmount the temptation and reenergize us for the spiritual adventure. This passage contains one of the most striking statements in the New Testament: "Indeed, the word of God is living and effective, sharper than any two-edged sword, penetrating even between soul and spirit, joints and marrow, and able to discern reflections and thoughts of the heart." The passage goes on to remind us that everything is "naked and exposed" to the eyes of God "to whom we must render an account."

In this reading, the "word of God" does not directly refer to Christ, the Word made flesh, or to the Bible, the written word of God, but to God's commands and directives that provide us with power and energy and also serve as judgment on our response to these divine gifts. It seems the author was concerned that Christian converts were losing their fervor, in danger of backsliding, maybe even returning to their previous practice of Judaism. He reminds them that the God who knows their embarrassing feelings and most secret thoughts will hold them accountable. Nothing escapes God's attention; everything stands under divine judgment. The word of God is penetrating and normative, sharper than a sword that cuts two ways.

As Christians today, what are we to make of this challenging passage? One possibility is to ignore it, as a harsh relic from an overly moralistic, heavily judgmental, long-abandoned form of Catholic piety. Another questionable option is to overreact in various ways: worrying excessively about possible sins, fearing God as a harsh judge, engaging in too much fruitless introspection, becoming overly self-critical, and indulging in undue anxiety over personal damnation.

It would be more fruitful to hear the epistle as a warning against any ways we might be tempted to backsliding or complacency: settling for mediocrity in understanding and proclaiming our faith; neglecting elements of our spiritual regimen (prayer, meditation, scripture reading, examination of conscience); premature acceptance of our faults as unavoidable; presuming our good works merit God's approval; growing weary in the struggle to live gospel ideals; and comparing ourselves favorably with other less virtuous Christians.

We can envision Christians responding constructively to the challenge of the epistle. A couple in an okay marriage could participate in a Marriage Encounter to enrich their partnership. A grandmother discouraged that her prayers for her alcoholic grandson have been ineffective could vow to continue asking God's blessings on him. A middle-aged man with a grade school knowledge of his faith could join the weekly parish Bible study. An elderly woman plagued with doubts about getting to heaven could meditate daily on God as a loving, compassionate, merciful, forgiving Lord. A concerned citizen worried about political complacency could decide to put more effort into getting out the vote in the next election.

What constructive step could I take to respond more fully to the word of God?

31. CELEBRATING MARRIAGE AS A PARTNERSHIP

Christians today who want to promote marriage as a partnership of equals must contend with the fact that the New Testament accepts some aspects of the patriarchal understanding of marriage common in the first century of the Common Era. As a prime example, we have the problematic verse, Ephesians 5:22–23: "Wives should be subordinate to their husbands as to the Lord. For the husband is head of his wife just as Christ is head of the church." Some evangelical Christians and traditionalist Catholics defend this teaching and try to live it out in their marriages. Most American Christians, however, find the whole notion of husband headship and wife submission repugnant and either reject it outright or look for ways to explain it away. The teaching from Ephesians is especially troubling as the "Me Too" movement brings to public attention numerous cases of powerful men taking advantage of women.

Let us examine the Ephesians passage in historical context. The author, probably a disciple of Paul writing in the late first century, lived in a patriarchal society with a generally accepted sexist bias. Although he wrote from a Christian perspective, which challenged some of the abuses of his day, he simply assumed that husbands were the proper heads of households and that their wives should respect this.

CONVERSION AS A WAY OF LIFE

Just as the biblical authors were influenced by their patriarchal culture, so we who read the scriptures today are influenced by contemporary developments and trends. Culturally, there is general agreement that women are worthy of respect and deserve equal rights, even if that ideal is not yet achieved. Theologically, Catholic scholars remind us that Christ's teaching on love presses toward seeing marriage as a partnership based on equality of the sexes and mutual respect of the spouses. Just as the ongoing reflection on the law of love eventually illumined the evils of the accepted practice of slavery, so does this same reflection illumine the lingering evils of patriarchy and highlight the ideal of marital partnership. Most Christians who have intuitively rejected female subordination in favor of marriage equality are on solid theological ground. The practice and teaching of Christ prompts couples to base their marriage on self-sacrificing love, mutual respect, and fundamental equality.

Let us consider this composite story of Jacob and Rachel, a couple who chose Ephesians 5:21–32 for a reading at their wedding Mass forty-five years ago. Influenced by their families, they both implicitly accepted that Jacob was head of the household. In their early years of marriage, they moved several times, each time choosing his career opportunities over hers. When they had children, she assumed most of the child-rearing responsibilities in addition to most of the domestic chores she was already doing daily. Rachel dutifully met her wifely responsibilities, attending to the needs of her husband and children.

Around their twenty-fifth anniversary, Rachel became dissatisfied with her predominantly patriarchal marriage. Jacob was quick to grasp the gravity of the problem, and together they sought advice from their pastor, who shared with them the Vatican II teaching on marriage as an equal partnership. With this in mind, Jacob and Rachel gradually developed new ways of relating to one another. He became more attentive to her needs, tried to do a bigger share of domestic chores, turned down a lucrative career move to have more family time, and supported her return to the job market. For her part, Rachel grew in self-confidence, was more assertive in her relationships, and found deeper satisfaction in her marriage. When they prayed together, they both expressed great gratitude for the new partnership they enjoyed.

What can I do to promote marriage as a partnership of equals?

32. DOING GOOD WORKS

Christians who are trying to work out a proper relationship between their faith in God and their responsibility to do good for others can find guidance in James 2:14–18, which argues that faith without works is dead and cannot save us. The author illustrates his point with an example. If a brother or sister in the community needs clothing and food and we wish them well but do nothing to help them, "what good is it?" It seems the author is responding to a misinterpretation of the Apostle Paul's teaching on faith and works. In his letters to the Galatian and Roman Christians, Paul insisted that they are saved by faith in Christ and not by following the Jewish law, for example, male circumcision and certain dietary restrictions. By the time James was writing, most likely in the 80s or 90s, Paul's teaching was commonly held in the Christian communities that had distinguished themselves from Judaism. It is possible, however, that some early Christians had misinterpreted Paul's teaching, claiming that he had emphasized faith alone to such a degree that he ruled out not only works of the Jewish law but also charitable acts in general. This would explain why the Letter of James puts such great emphasis on good works of mercy and compassion.

The issue of the relationship between faith and good works resurfaced in the sixteenth century, when Martin Luther, reacting to Church abuses and his personal anxiety over his own salvation, insisted that we are justified by faith alone and not by good works. Luther had little use for the Letter of James, calling it "a straw epistle," unworthy of serious theological consideration. The Council of Trent (1545–63) responded by condemning Luther's position and affirming that justification requires both faith and good works. For the next four centuries Catholics and Protestants were divided on this issue, both sides entrenched in their positions. This impasse officially ended in 1999 with the publication of the Joint Declaration on the Doctrine of Justification. Building on decades of intense theological dialogue, the Declaration stated, "Together we confess: By grace alone, in faith in Christ's saving work and not because of any merit on our part, we are accepted by God and receive the Holy Spirit, who renews our hearts while equipping and calling us to good works." While recognizing that differences of emphasis and explications still exist among Catholics and Lutherans, the declaration insists that they need no longer divide the churches. In effect, this suggests that Catholics and Protestants (other denominations have also accepted the declaration) can both read the passage from James fruitfully, incorporating it into their understanding of Christian faith and applying it to their spiritual journey.

Let us imagine some examples. A Catholic and Protestant blessed with a happy marriage could decide to enrich their shared prayer life by volunteering a couple of times a month to feed the hungry at a local food distribution center. A faithful Protestant quite familiar with the Bible, who has purposely avoided the Book of James, could include it in her daily scripture reading. A lifelong Catholic, who has a very private spirituality, could learn that working for justice is an essential part of practicing his Catholic faith. A committed peace activist could find new energy and motivation by deepening her faith in Christ the liberator of captives.

What specific good work would enrich my spiritual life?

33. INTEGRATING SCRIPTURE IN OUR CHRISTIAN LIFE

In 2 Timothy 3:14—4:2 we read, "All scripture is inspired by God and is useful for teaching, for refutation, for correction, and for training in righteousness, so that one who belongs to God may be competent, equipped for every good work." The author prefaces this teaching with a reminder that the Sacred Scriptures are capable of providing "wisdom for salvation through faith in Christ Jesus" and concludes the passage with the admonition, "Proclaim the word; be persistent whether it is convenient or inconvenient; convince, reprimand, encourage through all patience and teaching."

This passage prompts reflection on the role of scripture in our Christian lives. The Bible is the inspired word of God, the normative witness to God's plan of salvation, manifested definitively in Jesus Christ and his death and resurrection. At the same time, scripture is a human word, written by men (all males) who functioned not as secretaries or stenographers but as real human authors. As Christians, we believe that the Bible is inspired, meaning that the Holy Spirit guided the process of its writing and editing so that it is truly God's word for us. The Christian tradition has consistently taught that the Bible is inerrant, free of errors. However, modern scripture scholarship, reflected in Vatican II, has limited inerrancy to the religious and spiritual teaching of the scriptures, while recognizing some of its historical and scientific claims, implicit and explicit, are no longer credible; for example, we know today the Earth is not flat and is not some six thousand years old.

Scripture scholars can help us achieve a more accurate understanding of the actual biblical text. For example, most scholars today are convinced that 2 Timothy was written not by Paul himself but by a disciple or friendly commentator who framed it as advice from the Apostle to his younger colleague in ministry, Timothy. The experts remind us that the reference to scripture in this passage is confined to the Hebrew Scriptures, commonly known as the Old Testament, and does not include the New Testament. They tell us more about Timothy and his interactions with Paul, his mentor, which could help some readers get more out of the passage, for example, that he had a close personal relationship with the Apostle.

On the other hand, individuals can gain inspiration and insight just by reading the passage and reflecting on it without any scholarly help. A Catholic senior citizen could decide she is going to do more scripture reading. A regular at Sunday Mass could pay more attention to the Liturgy of the Word. A deacon could concentrate on preaching homilies based more directly on the readings. A parish religion teacher could resolve to check scholarly opinion before teaching his students the meaning and application of difficult biblical texts. A recently retired electrician could decide to spend some of his new leisure time reading through the four Gospels, a chapter at a time.

How could I make scripture a more effective instrument of spiritual growth?

Chapter Two

Moral Conversion

Moral conversion involves a change of heart so that we pursue goodness and virtue even at the expense of pleasure and satisfaction. Virtuous persons strive to live responsibly, following principle rather than expediency. They move beyond legalism, which settles for a minimal adherence to external laws, to a generous love that does not count the cost. At the same time, they also avoid the extreme of moral relativism, which denies the existence of binding moral principles and justifies a "do your own thing" morality. Virtuous persons make fitting moral decisions based on the call of God, the wisdom of the community, the knowledge of self, the needs of others, and the call of conscience.

Given our growing awareness of widespread injustice in our world today, the process of moral conversion must include participation in the great cause of liberating and empowering those constrained by systemic injustice. This moral responsibility is grounded on solid Church teaching. There is an essential connection between love of God and love of neighbor; sin has a social dimension, creating unjust institutions and dehumanizing systems, and working for justice is an essential element in spreading the Christian message. The moral virtues are like a second nature enabling individuals to do good spontaneously and instinctively with relatively little effort and much delight. Virtuous individuals draw on the moral wisdom of their formative tradition and contribute to the well-being of their communities. They cultivate the main moral virtues that enable them to act prudently, justly, temperately, and bravely, even in challenging situations.

Christians committed to moral conversion can find encouragement and guidance in the epistle passages in this chapter, especially since they were originally intended to help the early Christians develop the virtues needed for authentic Christian living. Those who engage these passages with an open heart and prayerful spirit are more likely to find applications for Christian living in our world today, which is so different in many ways from the first century and yet reflects common human concerns.

1. MANAGING OUR DESIRES

The deep longings of our minds and hearts can bring us closer to God, but they can also get out of control, leading us in destructive directions. Ephesians 4:17–24 has some good advice for us as we try to direct our desires toward God and away from idols.

In Ephesians, probably written to Gentile Christian converts near the end of the first century, the author writes, "I declare and testify in the Lord that you must no longer live as the Gentiles do, in the futility of their minds," adding "you should put away the old self of your former way of life, corrupted through deceitful desires." Rather, they should "put on the new self, created in God's way in righteousness and holiness of truth." The passage draws a sharp contrast between two ways of walking through life: the foolish way of futility and deceitful desires and the wise way of righteousness and holiness guided by the truth of Jesus Christ. Those who walk the foolish and deceitful path worship false gods, while those who walk the wise and truthful path worship the One True God revealed by Christ. Wise Christians put away the old self corrupted by futile and deceitful desires and put on the new self, empowered by the truth of Christ.

Circumstances change throughout history, but the problem of futile desires remains constant in human existence. We all have a deep desire for happiness. We seek a knowledge that is satisfying and long for a love that is imperishable. From childhood on, we tend to want what others have. Achievements are never totally satisfying and often serve as a springboard for new quests.

Our innate desires can easily get out of control, becoming futile and deceitful. We are tempted to create idols, to turn legitimate preliminary concerns into false absolutes. As human beings blessed with freedom, we can make a fundamental decision to pursue selfish desires and evil deeds. More common, our idol making demonstrates greater subtlety, for instance, failing to keep our priorities in proper order and making ethical decisions based on expediency rather than moral principles. Human creativity can make an idol out of almost any finite reality. In our culture today, this can include consumerism that puts too much emphasis on accumulating goods and having material possessions; sexual gratification that treats others as objects; partisan politics that makes party loyalty more important than serving the common good; and social media that impedes genuine conversation. The epistle encourages all of us not only to face our idol-making tendencies but also to rely on Christ to lead us to the truth.

We can think of people who have created idols and could benefit from reflection on the epistle. A hardworking sales manager who spends extra time on the job and much of his free time managing his stock portfolio, much to the consternation of his wife, could learn to put less emphasis on financial matters and more on family relationships. A young bachelor who brags about his many sexual conquests could start treating women with greater respect. A woman who has voted a straight party ticket for decades could begin to make discriminating decisions about candidates based on their positions on a variety of issues. A grad student who spends excessive time on his phone every day to the detriment of his personal relationships could limit his phone time and put more emphasis on face-to-face encounters with his family and friends.

How could I counter my own idol-making tendencies?

2. LEAVING JUDGMENT TO CHRIST

We must make judgments in life about persons, ourselves and others, but we can distort this process by, for example, judging others too harshly and ourselves too leniently. At a deeper level, we are tempted to judge God, to question divine providence, to demand an explanation of the evils of human existence. In 1 Corinthians 4:1–5, the Apostle Paul offers a helpful personal reflection on judgment. He begins by presenting himself as a servant of Christ and a steward of the mysteries of God. In the early 50s he spent eighteen months playing that role for the Corinthians, preaching the good news of the death and resurrection of Christ. After that he received a great deal of criticism, but this does not concern him in the least. He recognizes that he must account for his stewardship of the divine mystery, but he will be judged only by Christ and not by any human tribunal or even by himself. He says, "I am not conscious of anything against me, but I do not thereby stand acquitted." That judgment will come only at the end of time when the Lord returns and brings to "light what is hidden in darkness" and manifests "the motives of our hearts." Paul advises the Corinthians not to make any judgments until the end-time when "everyone will receive praise from God."

Paul's personal confession invites reflection on our own lives. Like the Apostle, we are all called to be servants of Christ. Our primary vocation is to be stewards of the divine mysteries, giving witness to Christ and his teachings in our own spheres of influence. One day, we will be held accountable for our fidelity to this vocation. After fifteen years of a mediocre marriage, Sam and his wife made a Marriage Encounter, which helped him embrace his vocation to be a better husband, an insight that enriched his marital life.

The passage also raises questions about various forms of judging and being judged. For Paul, the key is to realize that judgment is finally up to Christ, who alone knows the secrets of the heart and who will return at the end-time to judge the living and the dead. Our judge is the merciful Lord who told the Prodigal Son parable and forgave the woman taken in adultery. Being at the mercy of Christ is a comforting thought for many Christians. A good woman who suffered from scrupulosity, an excessive worry about sin, came to greater peace in her old age by trusting herself to the merciful Christ.

As Paul suggests, trust in divine mercy helps us deal with the negative judgments of others. Some criticism is constructive, and we should take it seriously. Other negative comments come from individuals who do not know our hearts and are in no position to judge us. A man who was in the habit of taking personally even vaguely negative remarks learned over time to consider their source and content more objectively. This progress also helped him to control his own impulse to judge others.

Finally, the Apostle cautions us about judging ourselves. We remain a mystery to ourselves. We cannot completely untangle the complex web of mixed motivations that drive our decisions. The examination of conscience is an important spiritual exercise, but introspection can become excessive, blocking a healthy spontaneity. A vowed religious developed a livelier spiritual life when she became less concerned about purifying her motivations and more dedicated to Christ.

What part of Paul's instruction on judging most requires my attention?

3. RESPECTING THE MATERIAL WORLD

It is possible to show disrespect for the material world in various ways: for example, polluting the earth, taking the beauties of nature for granted, and neglecting to care for our bodies. In the eighth chapter of his letter to the Romans, Paul provides us with a positive view of God's creation (vv. 18–23). He encourages us to bear our current sufferings because they are "as nothing compared with the glory to be revealed for us." He then goes into a discussion of creation, which "awaits with eager expectation the revelation of the children of God." The material world is intimately connected to the personal world. The sin of Adam not only estranged humans from God and one another but also from the natural world. Because of sin, "creation was made subject to futility." As Christians, however, we live in hope that creation itself will be "set free from slavery to corruption and share in the glorious freedom of the children of God." Paul describes this unified process shared by both humans and other creatures as "groaning in labor pains." It is as if the material world shares our longing for a final fulfillment. Through the death and resurrection of Christ, we already have "the firstfruits of the Spirit," and we now wait in hope for the definitive transformation: "adoption, the redemption of our bodies."

The reading reminds us of fundamental Christian truths. By virtue of Christ's redemptive work, we are destined for the life of heaven, which puts the sufferings of this world in perspective. The material world was created by God and possesses intrinsic goodness; however, its essential harmony was compromised by human sin; nevertheless, it will share in the final fulfillment of the whole universe. Through our bodies we are organically connected to the material world. We are saved by Christ as whole persons. We believe in the resurrection of the body and accept responsibility for caring for our bodies and for creation.

We can envision various responses by individuals who engage this reading as an important resource for spiritual growth. A man struggling for years with Lou Gehrig's disease could find renewed hope in the thought that the glory of heaven is so much greater than the sufferings of this earth. A climate change denier could be moved to read a summary of the encyclical *Laudato Si'* by Pope Francis and become an advocate of reducing carbon output. An overweight, middle-aged man could reflect on the essential dignity of the human body and adopt a regular regimen that includes daily exercise and healthier eating patterns. An English professor could recognize the negative effects of sin on nature and become more attuned to the imagery of storms, floods, and earthquakes in nature poetry.

In what specific ways can I show greater respect for the material world?

4. LIVING ACCORDING TO THE SPIRIT AND NOT THE FLESH

We all experience some tension between impulses to do good and temptations to sinful behavior. Understanding that tension and pursuing the good can be difficult. Let us examine the teaching of the Apostle Paul in the important eighth chapter of Romans (vv. 8–11). There Paul contrasts the flesh and the spirit. "Those who are in the flesh cannot please God." On the other hand, Christians who are in union with God through Christ live in the spirit. It is the Holy Spirit dwelling in Christians that enables them to be in union with God and to share in Christ's resurrection. "Although the body is dead because of sin, the spirit is alive because of righteousness." In other words, we human beings are subject to physical death because of sin, but, joined to Christ, we share in his victory over death and participate in his risen life, made possible through the Holy Spirit dwelling in us.

This passage from Paul is extremely hard to understand. The terminology is unfamiliar, and the argument seems convoluted. It helps to recognize the meaning Paul assigns to flesh and spirit. The word *flesh* does not mean our physical body, nor does it refer to our sexuality as has sometimes been assumed. It does signify all in our human nature that inclines us away from God. Spiritual pride could be as much a part of flesh as gluttony. The word *spirit* refers to all in our human nature that attunes us to God, which directs us to Christ, and that unites us with the Holy Spirit. Life in the spirit could be expressed through healthy physical exercise as well as a deep prayer life. Paul's logic may be hard to follow, but one of his main points seems clear: by avoiding the selfishness of the flesh and living according to the spirit, we will share in the new life of the risen Christ communicated to us through his life-giving Spirit. This interpretation connects the epistle with the gospel story of Jesus resuscitating his deceased friend Lazarus, the greatest of his seven miracles in John's Gospel. Christ is life-giving Spirit for all open to that gift. In turn, those blessed with the indwelling of the Spirit are called to live not in the flesh but in the spirit.

Let us imagine some positive responses to this epistle. A promiscuous young man who has always thought a strong libido was his greatest temptation comes to see that pride is really a more fundamental problem for him and often leads to his treatment of women as sex toys. A grandmother serious about coming closer to Christ discovers she makes more progress when she develops a deeper devotion to the Holy Spirit dwelling within her. A forty-year-old man unhappy with the direction of his life transforms his heavy, cross-centered piety into a resurrection-oriented spirituality, which helps lift his spirits and give him a new sense of hope.

What one concrete step could I take to live more according to the spirit than the flesh?

5. NOT GIVING IN TO DISCOURAGEMENT

It is easy enough these days to get discouraged just following the daily news, let alone dealing with the personal disappointment that affects us. As Christians we are blessed with resources to persevere in living the good news of the gospel despite all the bad news. The Apostle Paul makes this point in 1 Corinthians 1:3–9. Following the common letter-writing practice of the Greeks, Paul greets the Christian community in Corinth and thanks God for enriching them with eloquence and knowledge. He goes on to insist that "the testimony to Christ was confirmed among you, so that you are not lacking in any spiritual gift as you wait for the revelation of our Lord Jesus Christ." Paul concludes that God the Faithful One, called you to fellowship with Christ, who will keep you firm and irreproachable "to the end."

The Apostle knows that the Corinthian community is dealing with external threats and internal strife, but he wants to encourage them to live faithfully, confident that God has given them all the spiritual resources they need to persevere in doing good until Christ returns to complete his mission. They enjoy these God-given gifts and talents to contribute to the Lord's mission and not for their own competitive advantage within the community.

As we reflect on the epistle, amid our own threats and divisions, we can find a much-needed word of encouragement. The threat of nuclear war and terrorist attacks shadow the whole human family. Our country is divided by political polarization, economic disparity, social injustice, and diverse prejudices, including sexism, racism, and homophobia. Individuals are carrying heavy crosses, physical ailments, emotional distress, mental problems, and spiritual darkness. As we contemplate massive suffering and deal with our personal crosses, most of us know something of the temptation to withdraw from the public arena, to become cynical, to wallow in victimhood, to take refuge in passivity, to yield to discouragement, and to lose hope.

When facing this kind of temptation, we hear Paul reminding us that God gives us all the spiritual gifts we need to persevere in doing good. We have our faith in the Father who loves us unconditionally, in Christ who saves us, and in the Holy Spirit who guides us. We find inspiration in persons who have transformed their crosses into new life. For example, the Marine veteran who lost his legs in Iraq and now helps other veterans who are homeless; the former opioid addict who is happily married and volunteers in a drug rehabilitation program; the elected legislator who risks reelection by collaborating with a colleague in the other party; the wealthy woman who gives generously of her time and treasure to support a self-help program for the poor in her community; the parents who continue to support their gay son as he deals with homophobia; the black policeman from the inner city who always looks for opportunities to help his white colleagues better understand the black community they serve; the priest who continues to incorporate Catholic Social Teaching in his homilies despite the negative feedback from some of his affluent white parishioners. These examples support Paul's claim that God gives us the resources to persevere in living the gospel no matter the circumstances.

Who inspires me to persevere in living my faith in our complex world?

6. RESPONDING TO UNJUST SUFFERING

In a world marred by sin, some people suffer from unjust systems and unequal power relations. First Peter 3:18–22 deals with this kind of situation, offering encouragement to Christians suffering for their faith, most likely some form of social exclusion.

This text centers on Christ and his saving mission. Highlighting the efficacy of his death and resurrection, the author proclaims, "Christ...suffered for sins once, the righteous for the sake of the unrighteous, that he might lead you to God. Put to death in the flesh, he was brought to life in the spirit." The passage then makes some obscure reference to the risen Christ going to preach to "the spirits in prison" (probably the fallen angels). With God waiting patiently, Noah built the ark, enabling eight persons to be "saved through water." The author uses the Noah story to explain that Christian baptism is not a cleansing of the body but "an appeal to God for a clear conscience, through the resurrection of Jesus Christ" who now is at the right hand of God, where he reigns over the angels, authorities, and powers.

As we deal with the unjust suffering of life, 1 Peter, difficult to understand as it is, offers encouragement by rehearsing our fundamental belief in Christ, who leads us to God, who saves us through baptism, who conquers all the evil forces, and who now sits at the right hand of God interceding for us. As followers of Christ, we are called to follow his example even when it puts us in opposition to contemporary culture or provokes the ire or ridicule of others.

In the United States today, we are more aware of the systemic evil of sexism, as more women come forward with claims of sexual abuse at the hands of men. In many cases, these women have kept silent for years or decades out of embarrassment or fear of either rejection or reprisal. Typically, their assailant wielded power based on status, position, money, or influence. These women say they felt humiliated and demeaned by these unwanted and uninvited sexual advances, which range in severity from rape to inappropriate touching.

Some of the accusers have been unfairly branded as liars, betrayers, publicity seekers, and money-grubbers. All of them collectively have opened up the possibility of a new era: when men will be more restrained in their use of power over women; when women will be safer in their homes and worksites; when the abused will feel free to speak up and the abusers will face consequences; and when men and women can relate in healthier ways based on mutual respect. Some of these brave women have explicitly said their Christian faith gave them encouragement and strength to come forward. The eyes of faith can detect in all of them the work of the Holy Spirit, sent by Christ to transform evil into good and to extend the reign of justice.

What can I do to reduce unjust suffering?

7. MANAGING OUR TEMPTATIONS

We know times when some inner voice prompts us to do good, but we also experience moments when another alien voice calls us to act against our conscience, to pursue selfish interests rather than the good of others. In trying to understand and manage this inner struggle, we can find guidance in Romans 8:9–13. Paul uses the word *flesh* to designate all the factors in human nature that incline us against God and the word *spirit* for that dimension of the unified human person that is fundamentally open to union with the Spirit of God and, more broadly, all that attunes us to God. Employing this distinction, Paul reminds Christians, "You are not in the flesh; on the contrary, you are in the spirit, if only the Spirit of God dwells in you."

The Apostle uses the word *spirit* in a second way as God's own Spirit, who raised Jesus from the dead and who dwells within us. Today we would name this Spirit the "Holy Spirit," the third person of the Trinity. The Spirit unites us to Christ, who shares his risen life with us. Paul concludes the passage, "For if you live according to the flesh, you will die, but if by the spirit you put to death the deeds of the body, you will live." This reminds us that our everyday decisions have consequences, contributing to our fundamental option for either evil or good, for flesh or spirit, which ultimately leads to either eternal damnation or eternal life with God.

This fundamental spiritual insight could serve as a warning to individuals tempted to specific deeds of the flesh.

Kirk, an alcoholic, must be careful not to take even one drink of alcohol because one could lead to another, to a binge and a total relapse. When Jill is depressed, she must be extra careful not to overeat, which could set back her efforts to establish better eating habits. When Bill attends a social gathering, he must concentrate on being a good listener because otherwise he will dominate the conversation and fuel his egocentricity. Dan must always tell his wife about interactions with a female colleague at work as a way of keeping that relationship from becoming inappropriate.

What temptation of the flesh poses the greatest danger to my spiritual life?

8. LEARNING TO BE MORE PATIENT

One of the best-known passages in the New Testament is Paul's beautiful and inspiring hymn to love in 1 Corinthians (12:31—13:13). The first part emphasizes the immense importance of the gift of love: "If I speak in human and angelic tongues, but do not have love, I am a resounding gong or a clashing cymbal." The second section of the hymn personifies love, declaring that it is not jealous, pompous, inflated, rude, self-serving, quick-tempered, and resentful. The closing section emphasizes the enduring power of love. Prophecies, tongues, and knowledge will be "brought to nothing," but Love never fails. The passage concludes, "So faith, hope, love remain, these three; but the greatest of these is love."

Love is at the heart of the Christian life. We confess that "God is love" (1 John 4:8), the Source of love energy and the Goal of charitable activity. God so loved the world that he sent his only Son to bring us eternal life (John 3:16). Jesus instructed us to love God and our neighbor, indicating that our eternal salvation depends on how we treat the needy. Paul's hymn to love identifies the characteristics of true love as well as behaviors that love rules out.

Let us examine the first characteristic in the hymn: "love is patient." As Christians, we believe that God is patient with us, "slow to anger" (Ps 145:8) and always merciful to us as sinners. Patience is a virtue that inclines us to endure and remain unbroken by sorrow, hardships, and the multiple burdens of everyday life. Patient persons motivated by love maintain a calm spirit and a clear mind even in high-stress situations. Practicing patience does not mean overlooking evil or allowing others to mistreat us. The virtue does incline us to exercise restraint when provoked, thereby opening the possibility of reconciling a strained relationship.

Utopian expectations of human relationships tend to generate impatience. If we expect our friends to always be attentive listeners, we are likely to be annoyed when they are preoccupied with their own problems. We are more likely to remain patient if we accept certain realities: individuals do not marry perfect lovers; friends will at times disappoint us; some work colleagues will be difficult to get along with; children will make mistakes as they move toward greater maturity; other people have the right to pursue their own path in life; we are not perfect and our flaws irritate others; we should be patient with others because God is patient with us.

We can learn from persons who have accomplished good by practicing the virtue of patience: the wife who maintained her marriage by tolerating her husband's passionate love of football; the woman who kept a friendship intact by putting up with her neighbor's habit of bragging about her grandchildren; the electrician who gradually developed a friendship with a coworker who initially annoyed him; the demanding father who learned to respect his collegiate son's halting journey toward mature adulthood.

What next step could I take to become a more patient person?

9. PRACTICING HUMILITY

Most of us know something of the temptation to boast about our accomplishments and to exaggerate our successes to impress others. In striving to develop the virtue of humility, we can find guidance and encouragement in 1 Corinthians 1:26–31. There Paul reminds his Christian converts in Corinth of their lowly status in that society: not many were wise or powerful or of noble birth, as he put it. This assessment probably reflects the historical development of the Jesus movement, which did attract some prominent converts but mostly appealed to the poor and dispossessed. Paul suggests this is according to the plan of God who chose the foolish of the world to shame the wise, the weak to shame the strong, and those who count for nothing "to reduce to nothing those who are something, so that no human being might boast before God." When God accomplishes great things through weak human beings, clearly gratitude goes to the great God and not human agents.

The Apostle goes on to insist that it is by the grace of God that the Corinthian converts are united to Christ Jesus, who is the wisdom of God and the source of righteousness, salvation, and redemption. Paul concludes his argument, with a quote: "Whoever boasts, should boast in the Lord."

For Paul, boasting about ourselves is a radical sin, an illusory claim to autonomy, a false sense that we can save ourselves by our own resources. On the other hand, boasting in the Lord is the acknowledgment of our total dependence on God who alone can save us. The Christian tradition teaches us that humility is truth, accepting not only our complete reliance on God but also our own strengths and weaknesses, our virtues and vices.

In the United States today, most Catholics are among the privileged of the earth. Some of us, it is true, remain on the margins of our affluent society, but most of us are in the mainstream, with some holding high positions of power and influence. In short, most of us do not fit the profile of the Christians in Corinth. This makes the temptation to boasting more intense and the achievement of humility more difficult. Living a comfortable middle-class life can blind us to our dependence on God and foster the illusion of saving ourselves.

We know people who have appropriated various aspects of Paul's teaching. A veteran of World War II has always been grateful for the GI Bill that enabled him to get a college degree, find a decent job, and provide for his family. A politician has used her position of influence not for public acclaim but to serve the common good. A highly respected doctor has been careful not to boast of his accomplishments to relatives and colleagues. A divorced woman who made a successful second marriage has regularly thanked God for a second chance. A respected philosophy professor has tried to maintain a healthy perspective on his own importance by a nightly ritual: he gazes at the sky, reminds himself that there are some 100 billion galaxies each containing 100 billion stars, and praises the Creator for such an immense universe.

How can I limit boasting about myself?

10. ENHANCING COMMUNITY LIFE

Given the strong influence of individualism in our culture, we Christians have a special responsibility to insist on the social character of human existence and to do our part to

promote healthy forms of community life. Ephesians 4:30—
5:2 can help us fulfill this responsibility. It begins with the
striking admonition, "Do not grieve the holy Spirit of God,
with which you were sealed for the day of redemption."
Through the sacraments of baptism and confirmation we
have been sealed with the gift of the Holy Spirit. The Spirit
lives within us as a renewable resource for enlightenment
and encouragement. We have a deep personal relationship
with the Spirit, so close, the text suggests, that our sinful
behavior can sadden the Holy Spirit. Especially upsetting are
vices that disrupt community life as indicated by this verse:
"All bitterness, fury, anger, shouting, and reviling must be
removed from you, along with all malice." This admonition
can prompt an examination of any ways we today might
disrupt or diminish community life: troubling dispositions,
such as pride, arrogance, excessive individualism, indiffer-
ence, and harboring resentments; hurtful speech, including
gossip, backbiting, and slander; and omissions, for example,
failing to apologize, missing opportunities to encourage others, and withholding forgiveness.

The passage goes on to recommend positive behavior that enhances community life: "[And] be kind to one
another, compassionate, forgiving one another as God has
forgiven you in Christ." This advice is especially relevant in
our society, where traditional standards of civility and common courtesy are under attack. Even among persons of good
will, there are conflicts, misunderstandings, and hurt feelings that call for the kind of compassion and forgiveness
preached by Christ, who "handed himself over for us."

We should celebrate the community builders in our
midst: elected officials who maintain high standards of
civil discourse in serving the common good; neighborhood
leaders who bring people together to create a safe environment for children; teachers who foster mutual respect in the

classroom; pastoral leaders who promote dialogue and collaboration among various parish groups; police officers who put extra effort into fostering healthy community relations; coaches who teach young persons the value of teamwork; business owners who encourage their employees to respect minority groups; parents who teach their children to forgive their siblings for being imperfect human beings; and all the people we know who are compassionate to those suffering and in need.

What specific step could I take to enhance community life?

11. OVERCOMING TEMPTATIONS

As we struggle to manage our personal demons and persistent temptations, let us consider the helpful analysis offered by the Apostle Paul in Romans 5:12–19. In this section he explains that through the transgression of Adam, sin and death entered the world affecting all human beings. Paul goes on to compare Adam, "the type of the one who was to come," to Christ, the new Adam, who brought the overflowing gifts of acquittal and justification to all people, establishing a new era of abundant grace. In summary, "just as through the disobedience of the one person the many were made sinners, so through the obedience of one the many will be made righteous." In other words, Christ's saving grace, available to all, is more powerful and pervasive than the deleterious effects of Adam's sin. The Gospels make this point graphically by reporting the story of the decisive triumph of Jesus over Satan, who tempted him three times in the desert.

Today we live in the new era established by the death and resurrection of Christ. In this new creation, we continue to experience the struggle between grace and sin. In Paul's terms, the effects of Adam's sin are still operating in our world today. We are aware of our personal demons that war against our better nature. There is always the possibility that selfishness prevails over love. Human existence as we know it is flawed. Social sin, manifested in distortions such as sexism, racism, and consumerism, is a constant threat to a healthy human life.

At the same time, the new creation established by Christ is a divine milieu charged with God's grace. We know the impulse to do good, to follow our conscience, to choose principle over expediency, to follow the law of love, to heed the promptings of the Spirit, to put on the mind of Christ, to obey the Father. In addition, we benefit from institutions and systems that encourage personal virtue and promote the common good.

The good news proclaimed by Paul is that divine grace is always and everywhere more powerful than sin and all the evil powers. This is the best of news for all struggling against temptations: a collegian trying to limit his excessive use of the internet; an executive working to control her drinking; a husband attempting to avoid patronizing his wife; a grandmother striving to be less judgmental; a secretary wanting to curb her desire to expand her wardrobe beyond her means; a teacher fighting to avoid cynicism over the political situation. In our struggles against temptations, it helps to remember that Christ's grace is more abundant and powerful than all the Satanic forces.

In what temptation am I most in need of Christ's grace?

12. RESPECTING OUR BODIES

Our culture promotes questionable attitudes toward the human body that contribute to serious problems: sex trafficking young girls; widely available pornography; bulimic tendencies among young women; obesity problems for young and old, males and females; sexual abuse; and the hook-up culture on campuses. In 1 Corinthians 6:13–20, Paul presents a Christian understanding of the human body that challenges these cultural trends. He begins with a fundamental principle: "The body…is not for immorality, but for the Lord." He then offers reasons for respecting our bodies. The God who raised the crucified Jesus to life will also raise us to life. We should "avoid immorality" because our bodies "are members of Christ," meaning we become "one spirit with him." Given this close connection, Paul declares, "The immoral person sins against his own body." We are not only members of Christ's Body but also temples of the Holy Spirit, "purchased at a price." Our body is not an autonomous possession but is a gift from God. This fundamental truth moves Paul to conclude, "Therefore, glorify God in your body."

When Paul spoke of the body (*soma* in Greek is the basis for our English word *somatic*, as in psychosomatic diseases), he meant the integrated human person in our concrete physical dimension. He affirmed the human soul and the human spirit while insisting that bodiliness is an essential component of full personhood.

Paul's teaching could prompt individuals to develop a more harmonious and integrated Christian life. An overweight, middle-aged man could start exercising regularly, becoming a healthier, more energetic spouse, parent, and worker. A collegian prone to bulimia could reject unrealistic images of female beauty and come to greater acceptance of her God-given body, freeing her to adopt healthy eating patterns. A young man addicted to pornography could free himself for healthy relationships by learning to appreciate women, not as sex objects, but as human beings joined to Christ and animated by the Spirit. A collegian immersed in the hook-up culture on campus could find her way out by coming to see herself as an embodied spirit who treasures loving, romantic relationships more than mere bodily pleasure.

What can I learn from Paul's teaching on respect for the human body?

13. PARTICIPATING IN CHRIST'S COMMUNITY BUILDING

As we look for ways to bridge the divisions in our world, we can find guidance in Romans 15:5–7, where Paul asks God to grant them the grace to follow Christ's example by "think[ing] in harmony with one another," by living in "one accord," and by glorifying God in "one voice."

With the division between Jewish and Gentile converts in mind, Paul insists that Christ ministered to the Jews to confirm the promises made to Abraham, which included salvation for the Gentiles. Following the example of Christ, the Christian community should "welcome one another" for the glory of God.

Paul's call for unity is much needed in our fragmented world with its deep religious, cultural, economic, and political divisions. He provides us with a solid theological foundation for joining in the great task of overcoming divisions and bringing people together. We are all members of the one human family. The God who loves every person wills the salvation of all people. Jesus, the community builder, reached out to those banished to the margins and welcomed sinners. His death and resurrection unleashed the Spirit, who draws all people into a communion of love.

As Christians, we are called to carry on the community-forming ministry of Christ in our sphere of influence. Sue, a wife and mother of three teenagers, works hard to keep the family together and each individual happy. She and her husband talk regularly about shared approaches to raising their children. She sometimes initiates conversations with her spouse on how they can keep their love alive and continue to grow together spiritually. Attuned to the unique personalities of each of her children, she tries to make them all feel special. When disputes occur, she encourages them to work it out themselves, part of her overall effort to educate them to be responsible adults. Supported by her husband, she promotes the practice of sharing meals together at least once a week, with no cell phones allowed. She welcomes her kids' friends into their home and makes sure they have their own space. Over the years she has insisted that her family respect her time outside the family circle, including her part-time job as a secretary and her leisure time with women friends. Sue finds strength and guidance for living her vocation by participating in the Sunday Mass along with her husband and children who still attend regularly with her.

Sam, who owns a small advertising agency, lives out his community-forming vocation in the workplace. He knows all his employees by name; he spends time getting to know them and something of their personal lives and periodically consults them on how to make the business more efficient and productive. He purposely hires people of diverse racial, cultural, and religious backgrounds, convinced that diversity produces more creative ideas. During the recession, he kept some people on the payroll even though it hurt the business financially. Sam regularly prays for his employees, who are more like family.

How can I promote community in my own circle of influence?

14. LIVING OUR FAITH DESPITE TEMPTATIONS

We must live our Christian faith in the real world, which is a mixture of grace and sin, of trends in accord with the gospel and those opposed to gospel values. In Philippians 3:17—4:1, Paul speaks to this challenge when he warns his beloved converts about certain "enemies of the cross of Christ," who are causing problems in the community. It is difficult to determine who these enemies were. One possibility is that Paul was referring to the so-called "Judaizers" who challenged him by insisting that Christian converts follow the Jewish dietary laws ("their God is their stomach") and the ritual practice of circumcision ("their glory is in their 'shame'"). Whoever they were, they were headed for destruction because their minds were "occupied with earthly things."

The Apostle urges the Philippians to imitate his example and that of his faithful followers by standing "firm in the Lord." As those who have their "citizenship" in heaven, they are to await the coming of Christ who will change our "lowly body to conform with his glorified body by the power that enables him also to bring all things into subjection to himself."

This passage can prompt reflection on our fundamental outlook on life in the contemporary world. We can detect trends that are inimical to the cross: a rugged individualism that disregards responsibilities toward others; a consumerist mentality that thinks having things and accumulating goods is the key to happiness; and a one-dimensional humanism that views religious belief as dehumanizing. At the same time, our world manifests signs of God's grace at work: a commitment to human rights for all; an affirmation of religious liberty that enables churches to flourish; and a healthy volunteerism, prompting many citizens to assist those in need.

As citizens of heaven, we believe Christ will one day complete his saving mission, which means that all people will share completely in his risen life, that the good will

finally win out over all the evil forces, that the evolutionary process will reach its transcendent goal, that our deepest
longings will be fulfilled, and that the Lord will "bring all
things into subjection to himself."

We find inspiration in our fellow Christians who "stand
firm" and live their faith in our ambivalent world: those who
maintain a relatively simple lifestyle despite the glamour of
consumerism; those who are sustained by hope while grieving the loss of loved ones; those who devote themselves to
caring for others despite the temptation to selfishness; and
those who serve the common good despite the allure of a
self-centered individualism.

*What specific step could I take to live my faith more effectively
despite the temptations of the world?*

15. PROMOTING THE UNITY AND VITALITY OF OUR PARISHES

For most Catholics, their parish is the community where
they worship God, encounter Christ, and experience the
Church. We all have a responsibility to do all we can to make
our parish a credible sign and effective instrument of God's
reign in the world. Ephesians 4:1–6 encourages and directs
this responsibility, emphasizing the need to practice certain
virtues: humility that enables us to accept our proper role in
the community, gentleness that prompts us to treat others
with respect, and patience that helps us bear with the annoy-
ing habits of other members. The passage reminds us of all we
have in common as members of the Body of Christ animated
by the Spirit: "one Lord, one faith, one baptism; one God and
Father of all, who is over all and through all and in all."

The Church does not exist as an end in itself. It is the
sign and instrument of the kingdom of God. It participates

in the mission of Christ to unify the whole human family and to save all people. The Church carries out this responsibility through its members who live virtuous lives daily. We can all contribute to making the Church a more credible sign and effective instrument of the reign of God in the world by developing and practicing the virtues highlighted in this text.

Let us imagine a parish that manifests the virtue of humility: the secretary feels like she is an important part of the ministry team; the parish council members spend time eliciting advice from various segments of the community; the pastor thinks of himself as a servant leader called to coordinate the gifts and talents of the parishioners; the musicians see themselves not as performers but as facilitators of liturgical participation.

There are parishes that present a gentle spirit: the ushers make visitors feel as welcome as the regular parishioners; the pro-life committee promotes care for the most vulnerable, including the unborn, the extremely poor, and the dying; the bereavement committee provides free meals after the funeral for those who have buried their loved ones.

Patience is an important virtue for those committed to the long-term good of the parish: parishioners who give their new pastor time to adjust to the demands of leadership; the parish finance committee that works out a long-range plan for paying off parish debts; the pastoral administrator who gives the new secretary space to learn the job.

What virtue should I cultivate to promote the unity of my parish?

16. IMPROVING OUR PRAYER LIFE

We can all no doubt think of ways our prayers are deficient: allowing distractions to divert our attention; spending too much time asking for favors and not enough in praise and thanksgiving; saying too many words and not spending enough time listening; failing to relate private and liturgical prayer; expecting divine intervention without making our own effort; continuing to recite memorized prayers as we did as children without developing more mature forms; and failing to set aside time for prayer.

In Romans 8:26–27, Paul takes up the problem of our human limitations as persons of prayer, "for we do not know how to pray as we ought." We should not be overly discouraged by our limitations because we have the assistance of the Holy Spirit as Paul assures us: "the Spirit...comes to the aid of our weakness" and intercedes on our behalf "with inexpressible groanings." Biblical scholars inform us that the original Greek suggests that the Spirit identifies with our weakness and takes it on. The Spirit, who knows the will of God and lives in solidarity with us in all our limitations, serves as the mediator enabling us to pray. Paul concludes the short passage: "And the one who searches hearts knows what is the intention of the Spirit, because it intercedes for the holy ones according to God's will."

From the epistle we can extract some important theological themes and valuable spiritual advice. We human beings, though weak and limited, are called to holiness and a life of prayer. God, who knows our hearts, is worthy of praise and gratitude. The Holy Spirit, the mediator who identifies with our weakness, enables us to offer fitting prayers to God. In prayer, we are never completely on our own, dependent only on our own spiritual resources. The Spirit always prays in and with us. At the same time, we must cooperate with the Holy Spirit, doing our part to make our prayer time more fruitful.

Individuals could do this in several ways. A busy mother who often falls asleep trying to pray at night could try praying in the morning. An overworked executive who prays with many words could spend more time in silence listening to God. A coach who offers many prayers of petition for his family and players could say more prayers of praise and thanksgiving. A father of an autistic child, discouraged that his prayers for his son are never answered, could ask God for the gift of acceptance no matter what the future holds. A collegian who is often distracted at Mass could spend a few moments in prayerful reflection before heading to church.

What specific change could I make to improve my prayer life?

17. WORKING FOR PEACE AND RECONCILIATION

Given all the troubles and political, religious, and personal divisions in our world, we Christians are called to be peacemakers and reconcilers. Ephesians 2:13–18 highlights the role of Christ as the supreme peacemaker. The text uses the word *peace* four times. Christ, "our peace," established peace by breaking down "the dividing wall of enmity" between those who were "far off" (Gentile Christians) and those who were "near" (Jewish Christians). He preached peace to both groups and reconciled them by shedding his blood on the cross, creating "in himself one new person in place of the two." Through Christ "both have access in one Spirit to the Father."

The passage is recalling the great controversy of the early Church whether Gentile converts (those far off) had to embrace Jewish practices familiar to Jewish converts (those near). The author seems to argue that Jesus set the stage for settling the issue in favor of Gentile freedom from the law by his death and resurrection that created a fundamental unity among all his followers. Christ reconciled Jewish and Christian converts by reconciling both groups with God. He put the enmity that divided them to death, destroying its power to keep them permanently separated. His death on the cross established "one new person," and community united by the "one Spirit."

This story of reconciliation is of supreme historical importance, for it made possible the Christian religion as we know it today. However, it also contains lessons for us today as we deal with contemporary divisions among Catholics, Christian monotheists, religious traditions, cultures, political parties, nations, and civilizations. Dividing wells of enmity appear all over our common home, fostering hatred, injustice, and violence.

As Christians, we simply cannot accept these divisions as normal or unavoidable or permanent. Christ, our peace, preached peace and promoted reconciliation. By his death and resurrection, he definitively established a unity among all members of the human family, deeper and stronger than all the forces that divide us. Christ calls all of us to be peacemakers in our circles of influence. For us Christians, peacemaking is not an option but our vocation, our responsibility, our duty. Our faith teaches us that we are not trying to reconcile individuals and groups with nothing in common. We are, rather, trying to build on our common humanity as well as our shared status as God's handiwork and sinners justified by Christ.

To sustain our efforts, it is helpful to remember and honor the peacemakers in our world. There are the famous modern ones: Mohandas Gandhi, Dorothy Day, Thomas Merton, Daniel Berrigan, and Martin Luther King Jr. There are the peace activists who organize rallies, attend demonstrations, recruit helpers, visit trouble spots, and risk imprisonment. There are the faithful citizens who vote intelligently, write letters to their representatives, go to meetings, and send letters to the editor. There are parishioners who serve on justice and peace committees, encourage their pastors to preach on peace, and advertise peace events in the parish bulletin. There are neighbors who reach out to befriend those in the neighborhood who are different and subject to prejudice. There are family members who take the initiative to settle disputes and promote family harmony. Finally, there are those Christians who share in the peacemaking mission of the Lord by prayer and unnoticed acts of reconciliation.

What further step could I take to be a more effective peacemaker?

18. ENRICHING FAMILY LIFE

In our efforts to be a better family member and to improve the quality of our family life, we can find helpful guidance in Colossians 3:12–21. Using the image of putting on clothing, Paul, or one of his followers, as many reputable scholars claim, writes, "Put on then, as God's chosen ones, holy and beloved, heartfelt compassion, kindness, humility, gentleness, and patience, bearing with one another and forgiving one another." Extending the dressing image, he continues, "And over all these put on love, that is, the bond of perfection." Stressing the importance of gratitude, Paul adds, "And let the peace of Christ control your hearts," and "let the word of Christ dwell in you richly," preparing you to teach and admonish one another wisely and to pray together joyfully.

Historically, Christian teaching and preaching challenged the patriarchal patterns of family life that totally dominated the Greco-Roman world at the beginning of the Christian era. Over the centuries, progress has been made but problems remain. Domestic violence is all too prevalent, and the divorce rate is still too high, even according to the most conservative estimates. For many families today, the challenge is not just to avoid violence and divorce but to become a true "domestic church" that fosters spiritual growth of its members and contributes to the common good of society.

We can imagine individuals enriching their family life by practicing the virtues advocated in the epistle. A husband who resents the presence of his mother-in-law in his home could become more welcoming by developing the virtue of compassion, inclining him to be more concerned about her physical ailments. An older brother who regularly ignores his younger sister, could start practicing the virtue of kindness by listening to her when she wants to talk about her troubles. A wife who considers her husband spiritually inferior to herself could acquire over time the virtue of humility, opening her eyes to his unsuspected spiritual depth. A father who often speaks harshly to his collegiate daughter could grow in the virtue of gentleness, facilitating better communications with her. A son who chafes at his elderly father's dementia could work at developing the virtue of patience, enabling him to interact with his forgetful father without getting terribly upset.

What virtue should I develop to be a better family member?

19. DEVELOPING HEALTHY PERSONAL AND COMMUNAL RELATIONSHIPS

Forming healthy relationships and amicable communities is a challenging task in today's contentious world. The Christian doctrine of the Trinity can provide us with guidance and encouragement in meeting this challenge. In 2 Corinthians 13:11–14, Paul says, "The grace of the Lord Jesus Christ and the love of God and the fellowship of the holy Spirit be with all of you." An early indication of what would become by the fourth century the official teaching on the triune nature of the one God. It is typical of Paul's custom of ending his letters with a benediction, and it follows immediately after a series of final admonitions important for all Christians.

This relational understanding of God grounds Paul's admonition: "Brothers [and sisters], rejoice. Mend your ways, encourage one another, agree with one another, live in peace, and the God of love and peace will be with you." The fundamental problem in the Corinthian Christian community was the prevalence of divisive rivalries. Normal differences turned into bitter disagreements, hostile factions, and the breakdown of healthy community life. Given this situation, Paul encourages a more joyful, unified, and peaceful experience of genuine Christian community. Christians should rejoice because we are united to Christ who defeated death and all the dark forces. This requires mending our ways, softening our hearts, transforming envy into respect and selfishness into love. Christians should not tear down their fellow believers but should encourage one another to be faithful followers of their Lord.

They should be of one mind in their fundamental belief that they have been saved by the death and resurrection of Christ and in their commitment to live his law of love. Rather than accepting their contentious rivalries as normal, they should try to live in mutual peace and harmony, which is ultimately a blessing from God. We could say that Paul's admonitions are a call to live a trinitarian spirituality that reflects the dynamic communion of love shared by the Father, Son, and Spirit. Belief in the ultimately mysterious Trinity has an ethical dimension calling us to form loving relationships and harmonious communities.

Individuals could live this trinitarian vocation in various concrete ways. Lydia could apologize to her estranged neighbor as a first step toward reestablishing their friendship. Instead of always criticizing his collegiate daughter, Michael could encourage her by recognizing her virtues and praising her for her accomplishments. Jacob, who upsets his wife by flirting with other women at social gatherings, could mend his ways and pay more attention to his spouse. Beth, who generally tunes out the more radical voices on the parish social justice committee, could be more open to finding common ground based on commitment to Christ.

What concrete step could I take to promote understanding and peace in my relationships?

20. SEIZING CURRENT OPPORTUNITIES

Procrastination can retard our spiritual development and prevent us from accomplishing good things. In 1 Corinthians 7:29–31, Paul challenges our complacency: "I tell you, brothers [and sisters], the time is running out. From now on, let those having wives act as not having them, those weeping as not weeping, those rejoicing as not rejoicing, those buying as not owning, those using the world as not using it fully. For the world in its present form is passing away."

When Paul wrote this passage in the mid-50s, there still prevailed a general expectation that Christ would keep his promise and return soon to complete his saving mission. Paul, who shared this view, thought it should have an impact on the way Christians lived their everyday lives. Thus, he urged the Corinthians to act as though the end was near, that Christ's return was fast approaching. Men should avoid sexual relations with their wives. Everyone in the community should take a fundamentally different attitude toward the joys and sorrows of daily life. They should recognize the futility of acquiring more possessions and the folly of being overly concerned with the things of this passing world.

What can this passage mean to Christians today who do not expect the world to end soon? We could still appropriate the urgency of Paul's message. We do not have an unlimited time in front of us before we reach the boundary of death. Some things should be done soon, without unnecessary delay. Procrastination can give time for evil to develop and take hold. There is a Christian responsibility to seize the moment and to make the most of present opportunities. Paul's reminder that time is running out could propel us into constructive action.

For example, a couple in a troubled marriage could decide that now is the time to start professional counseling. A father who has been delaying the important task of sharing a Christian outlook on sex with his son could summon the courage and have that conversation. An elderly woman who has refused to face her imminent death could confront this reality and make the most of opportunities to reconcile some damaged relationships. A young man in a selfish sexual relationship, without any thought of marriage, could quickly be honest with his girlfriend so she can pursue more promising relationships.

Is there a serious matter that requires my immediate attention?

21. DEVELOPING THE VIRTUE OF PATIENCE

It seems that instant gratification made possible by modern technology has made us more impatient or reinforced our natural tendencies to be impatient. For those of us who would like to learn greater patience, we can benefit from reflecting on James 5:7–10.

Many Catholic scripture scholars think the Letter of James was written in the late first century by an unknown author who attributed it to James, the brother of the Lord who led the Jerusalem church until his martyrdom around AD 62. Chapter 5 reflects the common expectation in the early Church that Jesus would return soon to complete his saving work. Given his delay, the author advises patience, like the farmer who patiently awaits harvest time after the rainy season, because "the coming of the Lord is at hand."

The passage goes on to advise Christians to practice patience with their brothers and sisters, not complaining about one another so as not to be judged. The passage ends with an admonition to imitate the prophets as examples of patiently bearing hardships.

The Letter of James prompts further reflection on developing the virtue of patience. For most of us, it is not a matter of waiting patiently for Christ to return at the end-time. Our challenge is to remain patient as we face the delays and hardships woven into everyday life: long lines at the checkout lanes, traffic jams on the commute to work, lingering colds that last longer than expected, delayed divorces that elude a conclusion, enduring vices that frustrate spiritual growth, physical diminishments that accompany aging, prejudices that continue to plague our society, and terrorist threats that defy quick solutions.

In the Christian tradition, patience is a fruit of the Holy Spirit, suggesting that learning patience involves cultivating a deeper prayer life that quiets the agitated heart. A busy executive finds she is more patient with colleagues if she meditates for ten minutes before going to work. Thomas Aquinas taught us that patience, an aspect of the cardinal virtue of fortitude, enables us to face long-standing hardships with courage. A husband who practiced the virtue of courage throughout his life was able to sustain his care for his wife during the last two years of her life as she suffered the diminishments of Parkinson's disease. A mother maintained patient love for her rebellious teenage son by saying a prayer of gratitude every day for the way her parents were patient with her during her own turbulent adolescence.

How can I become a more patient person?

22. FACING THREATS TO OUR SPIRITUAL LIFE

We make our journey in life blessed and sustained by God's love and mercy, but we are also shadowed by the threat of temptation and sin. In this regard, the Apostle Paul in 1 Corinthians 10:1–13 warns us, "Therefore, whoever thinks he is standing secure should take care not to fall." Paul, who was a dedicated Pharisaic Jew before his conversion, uses the history of Israel to show that enjoying God's blessings does not necessarily ensure continued divine favor. His specific line of argument is difficult to follow, but in general, he recalls ways God blessed the Israelites in the exodus (e.g., guiding them through the Red Sea and feeding them with manna in the desert) and then notes, "Yet God was not pleased with most of them," because they grumbled and desired "evil things." The Apostle sees this history as an example for us Christians and as a warning against a foolhardy presumption that we are immune from sinful behavior.

As Christians, we are blessed in many ways: we are made in God's image, informed by divine grace, saved by Christ, and animated by the Holy Spirit, but we also live with the realistic threat of temptation and sin. As persons blessed with freedom, we find fulfillment by opting for good, but we retain the capacity to choose against our best interests. As unique individuals, we can construct a distinctive profile of the most serious temptations threatening us.

For many Christians, pride poses a serious threat to the spiritual life. Scripture warns us: "Pride goes before disaster, a haughty spirit before a fall" (Prov 16:18). The Christian tradition sees pride as the first of the capital or deadly sins, the root of all the other sins. Pride is an unreasonable love of self, an inordinate desire to exalt one's own excellence, an insatiable need for approval. It tends to obscure God's total sovereignty, to deny the talents and gifts of our neighbors, and to disregard our own faults. The spiritual masters suggest ways to reduce the threat of pride: meditating on the fundamental truth that we are totally dependent on God for absolutely everything, staying alert to the good in other people, recognizing our need for the love and care of others, facing honestly our own sins and faults, and cultivating a sense of gratitude for all the gifts of life.

For other Christians, however, the major threat is not overconfident pride but a lack of confidence, a false humility, an abiding sense of unworthiness, and a debilitating feeling of inferiority. This vice prevents individuals from recognizing the power of God's love, from forming healthy relationships, and from using their gifts to promote the common good. There are ways for Christians threatened by this kind of self-negation to make progress: meditating on the efficacy of God's grace, recognizing that there is justifiable pride in personal gifts and achievements, learning to accept honest compliments, pushing oneself gently to express ideas and opinions, and celebrating progress toward authentic humble confidence.

What is the most serious threat to my spiritual health and how can I best resist it?

23. APPRECIATING THE GOOD EXAMPLE OF OTHERS

As Pope Francis often reminds us, all Christians are called to be missionaries. We are all responsible for spreading the gospel of Christ. We do this best by setting a good example, by living our faith. We know this is true by recalling how the good example of others has been a positive influence on us, a gift that we should not take for granted. The Apostle Paul recognizes this dynamic in 1 Thessalonians 1:5–10.

Just a few months after establishing a Christian community in Thessalonica, Paul wrote a warm, affectionate letter expressing gratitude to God for their courageous efforts to live the Christian faith. In this passage, the Apostle praises those new Christians for their hospitality and especially for imitating him and the Lord, thus becoming a model for other believers in their region and beyond. These mostly Gentile converts "turned to God from idols to serve the living and true God" and now await the return of the risen Christ who "delivers us from the coming wrath."

In his high praise of the Thessalonians, Paul reveals the essential dynamics of the missionary thrust of the gospel. Christian faith is rooted in a personal commitment to Jesus Christ, the crucified and risen Lord, who lived a life of self-sacrificing love for the cause of God and humanity. Transformed and energized by his own encounter with the risen Christ, Paul carried out his mission to the Gentiles by striving to imitate Christ's love of God and neighbor. His good example gave credibility to his preaching, which touched the minds and hearts of the Thessalonians, who themselves became disciples of Christ, imitators of Paul, and models for other converts. Throughout the centuries, Christian faith has been passed on by believers who try to imitate Christ and find encouragement in the good example of other Christian believers.

We can imagine Christians expressing their gratitude for the good example of others. A cradle Catholic: "I am grateful to my parents, who daily practiced Christian charity, passing on to me a passion for serving others." A former agnostic: "My business colleague so impressed me over the years with her high moral standards and consistent care for others that I decided to investigate her religious tradition and eventually joined the Catholic Church, which has given me a faith perspective that satisfies my rational mind and challenges my selfish instincts. I expressed my gratitude to her by asking her to be my RCIA sponsor." Parents: "We were both inactive Catholics until our collegiate daughter got involved with her university parish and shared with us her newfound sense of meaning and purpose. We were so impressed with her personal growth that we started going to Mass again ourselves and have found great comfort and strength in returning to our Catholic faith. We remain grateful to our daughter for giving us such a great gift."

Am I grateful for those who have inspired my spiritual journey?

24. EXAMINING OUR CONSCIENCE

To get more out of the traditional spiritual exercise of examining our conscience, let us consider 2 Timothy 4:6–18, which portrays the Apostle Paul in prison, reflecting on his life and impending death. "I am already being poured out like a libation, and the time of my departure is at hand." Paul has in mind the Jewish ritual sacrifice of pouring out blood or wine as an offering to God. He sees his own life as a sacrificial offering to God, giving himself totally to his specific mission to bring the good news of Christ to the Gentile world, which cost him a great deal of suffering, including his anticipated martyrdom. He views his death as an eagerly awaited departure from this world and as a voyage to his heavenly home, like a ship leaving port for a distant land.

The Apostle goes on to borrow a metaphor from the world of athletics. "I have competed well; I have finished the race; I have kept the faith. From now on the crown of righteousness awaits me, which the Lord, the just judge, will award to me on that day." Like the runner who perseveres in a long-distance race and wins the laurel crown, Paul, who has remained faithful to his calling, has persevered in his mission, and has done his best to spread the good news of Christ, now awaits his heavenly reward. For him, this ultimate reward is a victory shared with all the faithful who have longed for Christ's return at the end-time. In the second part of this passage, Paul expresses confidence that Christ who "stood by me and gave me strength" in the past will "rescue me from every evil threat and will bring me safe to his heavenly kingdom."

We could use Paul's insightful prison ruminations as a guide for a personal self-examination, following his major themes to prompt some significant questions. His sense of being poured out like a libation: What role does self-sacrifice play in my life? Could I be more committed to my personal calling? Am I able to view the inevitable sacrifices of everyday life as catalysts for personal growth? Are there times when selfishness wins out over my commitment to serve others?

His outlook on death as a departure: Can I face the reality of my death? Can I talk about it with family members? Does the image of departure illumine my understanding of death? What will I miss most about departing from this world? Am I prepared for death?

His notion of life as a race: Does the athlete imagery appeal to me? In what way does my life feel like a race? What are the biggest obstacles that slow me down? What strengthens me to compete well? What spurs me on to complete the race? What role does a final reward play in my spiritual struggles? Do I find comfort in thinking of sharing the heavenly reward with my deceased loved ones?

His confidence in Christ's powerful presence: Are there times when I have felt energized or strengthened by Christ? How did I make it through my most challenging situations? Do I have confidence that Christ will continue to walk with me during the remainder of my journey? How do I try to open my mind and heart to Christ's example and teaching? Do I trust that the Lord will bring me safely to the heavenly kingdom?

Which of these self-examination questions deserve my further attention?

25. OVERCOMING INDIVIDUALISM

In American culture there is a strong streak of individualism that advises us to pull our own strings, do our own thing, and look out for ourselves. In contrast, Christian teaching grounds a more communal sense of the good life: we are social creatures who thrive in healthy communities; we are saved as members of the People of God; we are called to build up the Body of Christ; and we are instruments of the Holy Spirit who calls us to serve the common good. Christians who follow these principles can do their part to enhance their communal living. We see this theme in 1 Thessalonians 2:7–13, when Paul recalls how he and his fellow missionaries, Timothy and Silvanus, interacted with the Thessalonians who embraced the Christian faith. "We were gentle among you, as a nursing mother cares for her children." Paul and his companions developed such affection for their converts by sharing "not only the gospel of God, but our very selves as well." In those days, itinerate preachers were commonly provided with hospitality and sent forth with some recompense. Paul reminds his readers that he and his colleagues did not take advantage of those social customs but worked "night and day" preaching the gospel and plying their trades (for Paul, tentmaker), so as "not to burden any of you." Giving "thanks to God unceasingly," Paul insists that they preached not a "human word" but "the word of God, which is now at work in you who believe."

God used the generous ministry of Paul, Timothy, and Silvanus to help create a vibrant, influential Christian community in Thessalonica. Communal life, based on shared convictions, is typically enriched by dedicated members who give generously of their time, talent, and treasure. Self-sacrificing love that goes beyond normal expectations carries an inherent power of persuasion. Individuals who go the extra mile in serving others make gospel truths more credible. Sometimes magnanimous individuals inspire others to do more to serve the community.

Perhaps reflecting on the good example of generous individuals can deepen and expand our own sense of service. For many years, Millie gladly served as a focal point of unity for her extended family: sharing information, remembering birthdays, visiting the sick, hosting parties, attending important events (baptisms, first communions, graduations, weddings), and making sure everyone had a place to go on Christmas and Thanksgiving.

Distressed that their parish was not doing much by way of charitable outreach and working for justice and peace, Sally and her husband Bob worked diligently for more than a year to establish a parish social justice committee: gaining the support of the pastor, hosting open meetings to get parishioner input, developing a core group of supporters, sponsoring a presentation on Catholic social teaching, over-seeing initial meetings, helping to compose a mission state-ment, writing a bulletin insert on the project, and helping to surface ongoing leadership for the committee. This initial long, hard, work of Sally and Bob has paid off as the social justice committee now sponsors a food distribution center and supports the work of Bread for the World as well as other peace and justice efforts.

What specific thing could I do to build up community life?

26. LOVING OUR NEIGHBOR

In our culture, the word *love* is commonly applied to romantic relationships often with unrealistic expectations. By way of contrast, Dorothy Day, the founder of the Cath-olic Worker Movement, often spoke of Christian love as "a harsh and dreadful thing," quoting Dostoevsky. Actually lov-ing real, imperfect human beings is indeed a demanding and awesome challenge. In Romans 13:8–10, the Apostle Paul speaks about the centrality of this kind of love in the Chris-tian life. He tells us that the commandments prohibiting adultery, murder, theft, and coveting are summed up in the saying "You shall love your neighbor as yourself." This com-mandment, taken from Leviticus 19:18, is "the fulfillment of the law."

The word *love*, used five times in the passage, is a trans-lation of the Greek word *agape*, which is used in a Christian context to refer to the love God shares with us and, by exten-sion, the self-sacrificing love we offer to others. This love is not a vague feeling but a concrete effort to come to the aid of those in need, as suggested by the parable of the Good Samaritan. We are to do good for others, not simply because we like them or we owe them or we feel good doing it, but because this is our Christian calling to follow the command and example of our Lord. All other human beings qualify as our neighbor, including family and friends as well as enemies and those who are very different. True love is never self-satisfied. On the contrary, it recognizes the continuing call to deepen and extend our desires and our efforts to do good for others and to meet their needs.

We can imagine ways Christians could respond positively to Paul's message. A married couple who regularly pray together could do a better job of helping each other stay in shape through proper diet and regular exercise. A teacher who cares for all her students could give special attention to the boy with a learning disability. A concerned citizen who votes intelligently could get more involved in advocating for humane treatment of refugees and immigrants. A grandmother who is generally good to her grandchildren could spend extra time with her grandson who is struggling in high school. A factory worker who tries to be a force for good in the workplace could reach out to a fellow worker who is hard to get along with.

Is there a specific person who needs my love?

27. BRINGING PEOPLE TOGETHER

We are by nature unique individuals who need viable communities to develop and flourish. As Christians, we have a responsibility to help form healthy communities, starting with our own families. James 3:16—4:3 addresses this issue, beginning with the problem of wars, discord, and conflicts that disrupt community life. These disturbances are generated by disordered passions that disrupt our inner equilibrium and foster jealousy and selfishness. Foolish persons, driven by envy, seek what they cannot obtain. Employing "every foul practice," they "fight and wage war," striking at the foundations of a healthy community. Even their attempts at prayer are misguided and fruitless, as the reading suggests, because selfishness closes their hearts to God. Foolish persons pose a constant threat to community life.

By way of contrast, wise persons, guided by the gift of divine wisdom, help promote peace in the world by honest efforts to be gentle, compassionate, merciful, and righteous. The wise, blessed with a purity of heart, strive to do the will of God. They find practical ways to share love with others, to bring people together, to reach out to those on the margins, and to form inclusive peaceful communities. Wise persons enrich community life.

We can interpret this text as an indictment of others: family members who insist on doing their own thing, friends who are not there when we need them, colleagues who are hard to get along with, neighbors who take but do not reciprocate, parishioners who come to Mass but do not participate, public officials who serve their own interests instead of the common good, Church leaders who abuse and control, and world leaders who promote hatred and prejudice.

More significantly, the passage can prompt an honest examination of conscience, which may be painful but opens the possibility of real spiritual growth. Let us imagine how individuals could benefit from this spiritual exercise. A salesman who admits that he is usually friendly with customers but harsh with family members could find constructive ways to be a peacemaker at home. A mother who recognizes she is still smothering her collegian daughter could learn to treat her as an adult. A grandfather who comes to see that he favors his grandsons over his granddaughters could decide to pay more attention to the girls. A parishioner who confesses she does not contribute much to her parish could join the group that feeds people after funeral Masses. A citizen who admits he never votes in midterm elections could vow to do so next time. A Catholic who recognizes he has ignored a Muslim neighbor could initiate a conversation.

What concrete step could I take to be a more generous community member?

28. PRACTICING THE VIRTUE OF GRATITUDE

We all know the temptation to take gifts and blessings for granted, including the good example of individuals who have inspired our spiritual growth. Some background can help us appreciate Paul's teaching on gratitude in 1 Thessalonians 1:1–5, the earliest preserved Christian writing, from the year 51. In AD 50, Paul set out on his second missionary journey accompanied by Silvanus (Silas) and Timothy. They crossed the sea from modern-day Turkey to Greece where they first preached the good news of Christ in Philippi and then traveled about one hundred miles west on a major Roman highway to Thessalonica, an important commercial city and the capital of the Roman province of Macedonia. Paul spent, at most, a couple of months in the capital city, supporting himself by plying his trade as a tentmaker and preaching the gospel of Christ, strengthened by the Holy Spirit, as he notes in his letter. It seems from Luke's Acts of the Apostles that Paul was forced to flee the city before completing his work of establishing a Christian community, which would help explain why he so quickly sent Timothy back to see how they were doing and wrote them a letter just months after his departure.

In the beginning of 1 Thessalonians, which includes a conventional Hellenistic greeting, Paul gives thanks to God for all of his converts (mostly Gentiles), "unceasingly calling to mind your work of faith and labor of love and endurance in hope of our Lord Jesus Christ, before our God and Father." Throughout the letter Paul repeats his heartfelt gratitude for the way the Thessalonian Christians are living their new faith in Christ with perseverance and persistence.

We could use this passage as a catalyst for reflection on the virtue of gratitude, especially on being grateful for persons who inspire and enlighten us by living their faith. We know the temptation to take such good people for granted and to dismiss the importance of their virtuous living. It helps to recall the example of individuals who have risen above this temptation and practiced the virtue of gratitude.

Sue had a troubled adolescence during which she resented the efforts of her parents to guide her through her periodic escapades in the drug culture. Now a happily married woman and successful advertising executive, she regularly thanks God for her steadfast parents and has told them how grateful she is for their tough love that helped her get her life in order.

Mark, a married man who had had an affair with a colleague at work, was eventually forgiven by his wife, who acted out of her core commitment to Christ and his teaching. Unfortunately, Mark took his second chance for granted and did little to help develop a more equitable and loving marriage. Sometime later, when he was diagnosed with lung cancer, once again, his consistently loving wife was especially attentive to his needs. This time, Mark saw the light, recognized his amazing good fortune in having such a truly Christian wife, and vowed to spend his remaining years reciprocating her love and making up for his insensitivity.

Have I thanked individuals who have been a positive influence on my life?

29. STRIVING TO BE DOERS OF THE WORD

Most of us can admit something of the temptation to divorce what we have been taught as Christians from how we live our lives. In this case, James 1:17–27 can serve as a call to action. This letter was probably written in the late first century by a follower or admirer of James, the brother of Jesus and leader of the Jerusalem Church until his martyrdom in the early 60s. It puts greater emphasis on social concerns than any other New Testament writing, gathering a series of moral exhortations presented as wisdom instructions. The passage begins with a reminder that God, "the Father of lights," has given us "every perfect gift" and has planted his saving word in us, transforming us into "a kind of firstfruits of his creatures." The passage ends with a declaration that true religion is "to care for orphans and widows in their affliction and to keep oneself unstained by the world." In the heart of the letter, we find the crucial practical admonition: "Be doers of the word and not hearers only, deluding yourselves."

This admonition prompts reflection on possible ways of deluding ourselves by being hearers only. We can call ourselves Christians without leaving much evidence of this self-identification. It is possible to attend Mass without putting the message of the liturgy into practice. There is the temptation to affirm the law of love but to harbor prejudice against those who are different. We can accept that true religion involves attending to the needs of the most vulnerable, but exclude some from the list of the vulnerable, for instance the unborn, refugees, undocumented immigrants, prisoners of conscience, disabled veterans, and members of the LGBT community.

Let us envision believers who hear this epistle as a call to action. More Catholics could recognize that participating in Mass should lead to participating in the mission of Christ to humanize the world. Parents could do a better job of instructing their children in the ways of the faith by how they live and not just by what they say. Police could do a better job of representing the law by improving their relationships with the communities they serve. Elected officials could increase their effectiveness by making decisions based more on concern for the common good than partisan politics. Priests could deliver more effective homilies by practicing what we preach.

What specific step could I take to become a more active doer of the word?

30. TRANSFORMING THE POLITICAL PROCESS

In our country today, we are in danger of accepting our super-polarized politics as the new normal. Faithful Christian disciples who want to be faithful citizens have a responsibility to resist this trend and restore civility to the political process. On this moral obligation, the Apostle Paul, in Romans 12:1–2, reminds us, "Do not conform yourselves to this age." Because God has been so merciful to us, we should offer a sacrifice to God, not the animal sacrifices of the Jewish law, but the sacrifice of our bodies, our whole bodily existence in the world. We need a "renewal" of our mind so we can "discern" God's will, "what is good and pleasing and perfect." Paul is warning against simply accepting worldly wisdom, cultural assumptions, and secular ideologies. The Apostle wants us to concentrate instead on conducting ourselves in conformity to God's will. This requires prayerful reflection that relates the Christian message to real-life situations.

The world that serves as our habitat is itself an ambivalent mix of grace and sin. Some developments in our culture are in accord with the gospel; others are opposed. Sin gets embedded in institutions and systems, producing false consciousness. We are tempted to accept evil as normal, as just the way things are. The prophets help us name social sins: for example, racism, sexism, individualism, hedonism, and consumerism. Paul encourages us to discern the evil in these isms and to transform their negative energy into a positive force for good.

As a society, we are in danger of turning the social sin of political polarization into a new normal. There is a temptation to accept some questionable assumptions: that partisan considerations will always outweigh moral norms, that negative political ads are the only effective way to conduct a campaign, that civil discourse in the political arena is a lost art, that congressional gridlock is unavoidable, and that the search for common ground is a futile enterprise.

Ordinary Christians, however, are called to transform political polarization into constructive collaboration for the common good. A couple who split their presidential vote could have a reasonable conversation on the administration's policies. Catholics could follow the lead of their bishops and use the consistent ethic of life as the basis for judging candidates. More citizens could get involved in the political process. Elected officials could socialize periodically with colleagues of the other party. Voters could reward candidates who refuse to use negative ads to attack their opponent's character. Pastors could remind their parishioners that voting intelligently is a moral obligation.

What could I do to resist political polarization?

31. ACTING WITH COURAGE

We all know something of the temptation to cowardice, to be paralyzed by fear and intimidated by dangers. In this regard, let us reflect on 2 Timothy 1:6–14, when the Apostle Paul gives advice to Timothy his "dear child" (v. 2) and younger traveling companion on his missionary journey. Paul, who commissioned Timothy for ministry by the ritual act of laying on of hands, reminds him and us "stir into flame the gift of God," who "did not give us a spirit of cowardice but rather of power and love and self-control." He goes on, "Bear your share of hardships for the gospel with the strength that comes from God." The passage ends with the admonition to "guard this rich trust," the fundamentals of the gospel, "with the help of the holy Spirit that dwells within us."

Let us reflect on the admonition to overcome cowardice and bravely face the hardships of everyday life. According to traditional Catholic theology, fortitude or courage is one of the four cardinal virtues, along with prudence, justice, and temperance. As a virtue, it stands in the middle between cowardice or timidity, which allows fears to keep us from doing what is good, and foolhardiness, which leads us to take unnecessary risks and to rush into danger. Fortitude inclines us to act bravely in the face of physical, emotional, and spiritual dangers, and to persevere in doing good despite obstacles and hardships. The heroic martyrs provide inspiring examples of courage in the face of death, but all of us Christians have opportunities to practice fortitude in daily life. Courageous persons exercise patience by not giving in to anger or sadness as they strive to do good and grow spiritually. They persevere in acting reasonably despite failures and disappointing results. They continue to strive boldly for high ideals and lofty goals despite their limitations, by relying on God's assistance.

The stories of some courageous Christians have been widely reported. For example, Dorothy Day, the founder of the Catholic Worker Movement, frequently demonstrated for justice even though it meant going to jail. Óscar Romero, archbishop of San Salvador, spoke up for the poor and persecuted in his country, fully aware that it could cost him his life, as happened when he was felled by an assassin's bullet while presiding at liturgy. Dietrich Bonhoeffer, the outstanding Lutheran theologian, returned to Germany to join the resistance against Hitler, who gave the order to execute him shortly before the end of the war.

We can also think of ordinary believers who courageously persevered in doing good despite dangers and hardships. The young mother who endured painful bone marrow transplants so she could have a few more years to raise her two children. The gay collegian who summoned the courage to tell his father about his sexual orientation, expecting the harsh reaction that he indeed had to endure. The pastor of an affluent parish who publicly supported efforts to integrate the all-white neighborhood, knowing it would alienate some parishioners and hurt the collection.

How could I exercise the virtue of fortitude in my life?

32. FOLLOWING SCRIPTURAL ADVICE

We can find a lot of good practical advice for living the Christian life in the New Testament pastoral letters. For example, in 1 Timothy 6:11–16, the author charges us before God, the King of kings, and Christ Jesus "to keep the commandment without stain or reproach." He calls us to pursue righteousness by acting justly in our complex world, to devote ourselves to doing the will of God in our daily lives, to trust that God remains with us on our earthly journey, to love our neighbors by treating them with respect and compassion, to remain patient with loved ones over the long haul, and to be gentle with the needy and vulnerable. The author urges us to "compete well for the faith," recalling an athlete putting forth maximum effort to win the prize. That prize is the eternal life with God initiated by our baptism. We can persevere in the race, confident that Christ will complete his saving work, manifesting God as the King of kings and the Lord of lords, who "dwells in unapproachable light, and whom no human being has seen or can see. To him be honor and eternal power. Amen."

Let us imagine Christians who have taken seriously the sound advice of this passage. A baby boomer who for years concentrated on keeping the Ten Commandments committed himself to following Christ's command to love our neighbor, an ideal that is far more demanding. A retired executive who resisted Catholic social teaching and its application to current issues most of her life recognized over a period of time that it not only helps her understand contemporary issues but also provides a compelling reason for participating in the parish social justice committee. A grad student who considered his job options mostly in terms of how much money they would pay was persuaded by a trusted religious sister to think more in terms of a career that would be personally fulfilling and help make the world a better place. An elderly grandmother who doubted her usefulness to others in her declining years came to recognize that the merciful God, who blessed her with many happy years as a stay-at-home mom, continues to walk with her giving deeper significance to all she does in her remaining days. A disgruntled bus driver who dreaded his daily run because some of his riders were rude found new enthusiasm for his job when he practiced Christ's admonition to love our enemies by being extra kind to all his passengers, especially the most troublesome. A wife who was often upset by her husband's procrastination kept her marriage intact by concentrating on the good qualities of her loving spouse and being patient with his limitations. A stern father discovered over time that his children responded better to gentleness.

Which bit of advice in this passage do I most need to make spiritual progress?

33. PROMOTING ECONOMIC JUSTICE

James 5:1–6 has harsh words for the wealthy who have acted unjustly: "Come now, you rich, weep and wail over your impending miseries," graphically described as "rotted" wealth, "moth-eaten" clothes, "corroded" gold and silver, and burnt flesh. The wealthy have acted unjustly, withholding wages from their farm workers. God hears the cries of the defrauded and declares to the wealthy, "You have lived on earth in luxury and pleasure; you have fattened your hearts for the day of slaughter," presumably the final judgment when their greed and injustice will condemn them.

We all hear the scriptures in the context of our own social, economic, political, and religious locations. Those who are economically deprived in various ways (whether indigent, poor, unemployed, underemployed, victims of injustice) may well interpret the epistle as confirmation that God hears their prayers, that justice will prevail, and that oppressors will be held accountable. For them, the reading is good news, a liberating message, a sign of hope, a call to action, a promise of divine help in the struggle for greater justice.

For those of us who are in more favorable financial situations (whether comfortable, well-off, financially secure, affluent, or wealthy) the reading may prompt reflection on various financial issues, such as wealth disparity, economic privilege, just distribution of goods, and charitable giving. In pondering these and other issues, it is important to remember that the epistle does not condemn simply having many possessions or being wealthy. The wealthy are chastised for being greedy and for treating others unjustly to their own financial benefit. They have foolishly put their trust in wealth, failing to recognize the impermanence of material goods. They have accumulated more things than they can use and have failed to share their abundance with those in need. They have incurred divine judgment because they have worshiped a false god.

Let us imagine ways that Christians today, blessed with various degrees of financial success, could meet the challenge presented by the Letter of James. A successful corporate executive could decide to give a greater share of her substantial yearly income to charitable causes. A frugal retired electrician, who can enjoy a comfortable retirement with his wife and family, could make prayers of gratitude a more important part of his Sunday worship. A male employee could stand up for his female colleagues asking for equal pay. A wealthy widower could set up a foundation in his wife's memory to help promote literacy among disadvantaged youth. A financially secure couple could take steps to simplify their lifestyle. We could all do an honest self-examination on ways, perhaps subtle, that we fall prey to the allure of consumerism.

What step can I take to use my financial blessings more constructively?

34. OVERCOMING RACISM

In trying to understand the historical roots of slavery, our nation's original sin, we can examine the brief letter the Apostle Paul wrote to Philemon (vv. 7–22), the head of a house church in the Colossae region (modern-day Turkey).

CONVERSION AS A WAY OF LIFE

In his letter, Paul says he is sending Onesimus, a runaway slave, back to his master Philemon, hoping that he will free him and treat him like a brother in the Lord. It is likely that Paul had a hand in converting Onesimus to Christianity since he refers to him as "my child." The Apostle's appeal to Philemon is astute and personal: "So if you regard me as a partner, welcome him as you would welcome me."

The passage raises the troublesome issue of Christian approaches to the dehumanizing institution of slavery. At the time of Paul, the economy of the Roman Empire was based on having a large number of slaves laboring as miners, construction workers, and rowers on ships. Some slaves were better off than others, working as household domestics or as administrators of their master's estates. To Paul's credit, he did propose a theological justification for freeing slaves and treating them with dignity based on their relationship with their brother Christ in whom there is neither slave nor free, but all are one. At the same time, Paul clearly did not challenge the institution of slavery but seemed to accept it as part of the social order. One possible justification for his insensitivity is that he expected Christ to return soon to complete the establishment of the kingdom of justice, so that there was no real need to challenge the existing social order. Another possibility is that the Apostle simply did not recognize the social implications of his insightful theological position that all people are fundamentally equal in Christ.

We do know that historically Christians have used Paul's silence to defend the institution of slavery, including the chattel slavery prevalent in the United States into the middle of the nineteenth century. Even today, there are white nationalists who continue to use isolated scripture quotes to justify their prejudice against black Americans.

However, all mainline churches have finally come to see the social implications of Paul's teaching that Christ is brother to all human beings. This is a prime example of an authentic development of doctrine, the gradual realization of the deeper meaning and proper application of the teachings of Jesus and the biblical witness to him. In their 2018 pastoral letter against racism, "Open Wide Our Hearts," the American bishops confessed the complicity of the Catholic Church in the slave trade as well as the failure of American bishops to oppose slavery. They went on to name racism as our original sin and declared it to be a "life issue," along with abortion and euthanasia, which violates the inherent dignity of each person. They end their letter by adopting the words of the Apostle Paul, who taught us to be courageous and strong: "Your every act should be done with love" (1 Cor 16:14).

What can I do to overcome racism?

Chapter Three

Religious Conversion

Our efforts to become wise and virtuous persons never totally succeed. We inevitably disappoint ourselves and fail to achieve our highest ideals. We live in a world in which the power of evil is all too evident and at times seems to be growing. Our culture creates attractive idols, turning preliminary concerns for pleasure, power, and prestige into absolute concerns that demand our time and energy. Our innate drive for authentic self-transcendence seldom proceeds easily and smoothly and is always threatened by personal and social evil.

Religious conversion is a process of making God our ultimate concern and rejecting all societal and cultural idols. True believers maintain the convictions that human existence is meaningful despite all the evident absurdity surrounding us and that love will triumph over all the evil threatening us. Authentic believers sense that the mystery encompassing us is benign and gracious even while remaining incomprehensible and inexhaustible.

Religious conversion involves falling in love with the God who first loved us. We are in the gracious hands of God who always loves us unconditionally and never tires of forgiving us. We are called to deepen and extend our love for God by sharing that great gift with others. Faithful believers rely on the power of prayer to reject idols, to keep their priorities in proper order, and to love God and neighbor daily.

The meditations in this chapter invite us in various ways to keep striving for high ideals, for genuine spiritual development, for a more inclusive love of neighbor, and for a deeper love of God, despite our personal limitations and social pressures.

1. UNDERSTANDING GOD'S POWER

The dark forces in the world can seem overwhelming: terrorism, war, disease, natural disasters, mass shootings, domestic violence, and personal demons. As believers, we naturally turn to God, the omnipotent Lord, for help, but in doing so it is important to understand the nature and limits of the divine power. In Ephesians 1:17–23, there is a passage that provides some insight on this difficult question.

This passage, probably written in the 90s by one of Paul's most eloquent disciples, is cast in the form of a prayer, with a series of petitions asking God for the gift of wisdom, "resulting in knowledge" of "the God of our Lord Jesus Christ, the Father of glory." The author prays, "May the eyes of [your] hearts be enlightened" so we may know God's surpassing power and "great might," which gives us hope that we will share in the inheritance of the "holy ones." God's mighty power raised Christ from the dead and seated him at his right hand, where he reigns over all creatures placed "beneath his feet." As head of the Church, his Body, Christ's glory "fills all things in every way." The author of Ephesians, "Paul's best disciple," prays that we will have deep personal knowledge and appreciation of God's great might, which will inspire and guide our everyday Christian life.

It is important that we have a proper Christian understanding of God's power, which is always informed by divine love. God's omnipotence is not coercive or harsh. It respects the dynamics of the evolving material world and the fundamental freedom of the human beings created in the divine image. Divine power is loving, compassionate, and forgiving, always empowering us to develop our potential and contribute to the common good. We get our best sense of God's power by reflecting on the story of Jesus, who trusted his Father's loving power to the point of death that led to his resurrection and ascension to God's right hand. Christ's victory over death reminds us that God is our mighty champion, more powerful than all the dark forces that assail us.

The epistle's prayerful reflection on God's power could serve as good news for many people: those who need hope in their struggle against addictions; those who are tempted to give up on prayer because it is not helping; those who have encountered the scholarly claim that Jesus was a weak, vacillating figure who put too much emphasis on being meek; those who buy into the myth that guns are the source of power; those tempted to become cynical about the partisan political divide in our country; those fatigued by the heavy burden of caring for the sick and elderly; those weakened by the misconception that the ascended Christ left us alone; those who are at the mercy of powerful social forces; those brought to despair by chronic pain; and those who no longer seek truth and wisdom. We can all benefit from greater trust in God's merciful compassionate power.

What is my own conception of God's power and how could it be refined?

2. THANKING GOD FOR BLESSINGS

Colossians 1:9–14 reminds us to thank God for specific blessings. "[Let us give] thanks to the Father, who has made you fit to share in the inheritance of the holy ones in light. He delivered us from the power of darkness and transferred us to the kingdom of his beloved Son, in whom we have redemption, the forgiveness of sins."

Almighty God is the source of our very existence as human beings and of all our blessings. The Gracious One is not only the giver of all good gifts but is also the gift given. Grace is not a finite thing but the divine presence living within us, divinizing us, conforming us to Christ so that the Holy Spirit can inhabit our body and soul. God's self-communication creates and sustains us. Our debt of gratitude for such a free unearned gift is infinite, beyond our comprehension, and beyond our capacity to repay. Nevertheless, an authentic sense of gratitude to God calls for a life of thanksgiving, a life of self-sacrificing love, punctuated by prayers of gratitude.

The Colossians passage highlights three specific divine gifts. First, we share in "the inheritance of the holy ones in light," suggesting that we are destined to become part of the great Communion of Saints, where we join our deceased loved ones in heaven, find complete fulfillment of our deepest longings, live with God forever, and rejoice with Christ our King at the heavenly banquet.

Second, we have been delivered from "the power of darkness," indicating that the Father's gift of divine grace is more powerful than all the dark forces that assail us as we walk this earth; that Christ's power to heal and reconcile is stronger than the roaring lions that attack and scatter; and that the wisdom of the Holy Spirit will prevail over the deceit of the evil one.

Finally, we have been "transferred" to the kingdom of Christ, meaning that we now live in a world where the eyes of faith can detect signs of God's compassionate presence and the Holy Spirit's liberating activity.

We can all benefit from recognizing the surpassing power of God's gifts to us: those anxious about salvation for themselves and loved ones who are now silent; those who feel overwhelmed by the global evil of terrorism, violence, and war; those distressed by polarized politics, governmental gridlock, and attacks on fundamental truth; those discouraged by the persistence of racism, sexism, and homophobia; those despondent over Church scandals; and all of us who tend to take so many blessings for granted and spend so little time on prayers of gratitude.

What specific steps could I take to develop the virtue of gratitude?

3. WALKING BY FAITH, NOT BY SIGHT

On our earthly journey we do not control our origins or the final boundary of death. We cannot be certain about what tomorrow will bring, how relationships will impact our lives. In this sense we always walk in the dark valley even in our moments of great joy that may pass quickly. The Apostle Paul deals with this stark reality in the very personal 2 Corinthians 5:6–10.

In this passage, Paul contrasts life on this earth, away from the Lord, with life in the new world, at home with the

Lord. Although Paul would prefer being at home with Christ in the final fulfillment we call heaven, he aspires to please the Lord by acting courageously during his earthly journey, so that he will receive his recompense when he "appear[s] before the judgement seat of Christ."

Paul speaks for all Christians when he says, "We walk by faith, not by sight." We all know something about limited vision as we wend our way through life. Our personal perspectives on important issues can blind us to other legitimate viewpoints. We make many decisions without being able to foresee all the consequences. We cannot always be sure that our altruistic motivations for doing good are not shadowed by hidden self-interest. The future remains fundamentally unknowable, always subject to unforeseen developments. The inevitability of death does not make it predictable or transparent.

For us Christians, to walk by faith means we trust that our journey is not absurd but ultimately meaningful. God our Father is the source and goal of our sojourn on this earth. When we walk in the dark valley, Christ is at our side as our companion and model. Our eyes of faith detect the presence of the Holy Spirit in the joys and sorrows of everyday life. The doctrinal and moral teachings of the Church, accepted in faith, provide guidance as we encounter the complex challenges of the contemporary world. Our hope in a final fulfilling goal of our earthy pilgrimage encourages us to trust in our ongoing struggle against all the dark forces.

We can find inspiration in people who walk by faith and not by sight. The mother who continues to pray for her alcoholic son even though he has relapsed so often. The philosophy professor who continues to practice her Catholic faith even though she cannot resolve all the intellectual doubts that assail her. The peace activist who continues to advocate for a just resolution of the conflict between Israelis and Palestinians despite seemingly insurmountable obstacles. The veteran who remains committed to his wife and children despite the physical and emotional wounds incurred in battle.

Can I think of a specific situation when God has empowered me to walk by faith and not by sight?

4. MEETING OUR RESPONSIBILITY TO PREACH THE GOSPEL

Not many lay Catholics think of themselves as preachers of the gospel. In fact, some are turned off by the aggressive proselytizing of evangelical Christians. We can get some perspective on this by considering the Apostle Paul's personal reflection in 1 Corinthians 9:18–23, where he defends his practice of not charging for his preaching the gospel. During his eighteen months in Corinth, he supported himself by making tents for travelers. Evidently some of his critics claimed that he did not accept payment for his services because he was not a true apostle and did not deserve recompense.

This epistle is part of Paul's passionate defense of his freely offered preaching ministry. He insists that God has imposed on him the obligation to preach the gospel, a type of stewardship entrusted to him, which he willingly accepts. Offering the gospel free of charge is part of his strategy to win over as many as possible. The Apostle explains, "To the weak I became weak, to win over the weak." His real recompense for preaching is not payment or human praise but to have a share in the beauty and power of the gospel of Christ, the good news he proclaims.

Let us reflect on Paul's fundamental assertion that he is

under an obligation to preach the gospel. We could say the same about ourselves. By virtue of our baptism, we share in the mission of Christ to spread the reign of God in the world. We are co-responsible for building up the Body of Christ. As members of the Church, we share in its worldwide mission to preach the gospel to all people. Sharing in the mission of Christ is not optional. It is an obligation rooted in the very essence of Christian belief and practice.

We meet this obligation by living our faith in our own sphere of influence. Most of the time, example is a more effective way of proclaiming the good news than words, although saying the name of Jesus at the right time, when others are open to hearing it, can multiply the positive effects of good example. With Paul, we can affirm that God has entrusted us with stewardship of Christ's gospel, making us responsible for its integrity and expansion.

We can find inspiration in Christians who effectively proclaim the good news in their sphere of influence. A mother who treated each one of her five children in a uniquely loving way enabled them to develop self-confidence and to get a glimpse of God's unconditional love. A small business owner, who suffered financial loss by keeping his employees on the payroll in challenging times, exemplified the gospel admonition to go the extra mile. A wife, who lavished compassionate care on her husband, suffering for years from dementia, proclaimed by example Christ's gospel of generous love. A doctor, who talked openly about his Christian faith and led medical mission trips to Latin American countries for over a decade, preached the social gospel by word and deed to the students who accompanied him and the poor people served.

How can I spread the gospel more effectively?

121

5. PRACTICING THE UNIVERSAL PRIESTHOOD

We are still appropriating the teachings of Vatican II, including its emphasis on the universal priesthood of Christ shared by all the baptized. It helps to recall the scriptural basis for this crucial doctrine in 1 Peter, which presents Christ as the "cornerstone" of the "spiritual house," the solid foundation and unifying force for the Christian community. It then describes the followers of Jesus as "living stones" sharing the life of Christ, forming with the cornerstone a "spiritual house." We are "a holy priesthood," able "to offer spiritual sacrifices acceptable to God through Jesus Christ." God has called us "out of darkness into his wonderful light." We are "a chosen race, a royal priesthood, a holy nation, a people of his own" with the responsibility to worship God and form a community with Christ (1 Pet 2:4–9).

Drawing on this passage from 1 Peter, Vatican II put great emphasis on the universal priesthood. By virtue of baptism, we all share in the priesthood of Christ, participating in the Eucharist and living the active life of charity in the world.

As a result of this conciliar teaching, lay ministry in the United States has flourished as never before. Furthermore, Pope Francis has put renewed emphasis on the Church as the People of God and on the baptismal priesthood, setting the stage for more Catholics to get involved in the internal life of the Church and its mission to care for marginalized people and for our common home.

Future progress can build on the good example of individuals who learn to appreciate and live their baptismal priesthood. For example, Alex originally got involved in his parish when his pastor asked him to serve on the newly formed parish liturgy committee. Although he knew nothing about liturgy, he agreed because he could not say no to his pastor. Being a conscientious man, he began a systematic effort to develop a more mature understanding of his faith. He acquired the *Catechism*, which he used to find answers to questions as they arose. He attended a lecture that taught him that his baptism made him a member of the universal priesthood of Christ with a vocation to become holy and to spread the kingdom in the world. His whole attitude toward living his Christian faith changed, which enriched his participation on the liturgy committee, especially when he saw the participation at Mass improving.

Later, he ran for a position on the parish council, not because the pastor asked him, but because he saw serving on the council as an effective way of living his baptismal priesthood. After his term was over, Alex, wanting to stay involved, joined the parish social justice committee, which moved him to learn more about Catholic social teaching. We can hope that Alex's story, and the good example of so many involved Catholics, will inspire others to take more seriously their vocation as members of Christ's priesthood.

What concrete step can I take to live my baptismal priesthood?

6. STRIVING FOR SPIRITUAL GROWTH

For those tempted to spiritual complacency, lethargy, and mediocrity, the Apostle Paul offers encouragement for us as he did for the Christian community in Thessalonica, around the year AD 50. "May the Lord make you increase and abound in love for one another and for all…to strengthen your hearts, to be blameless" before God at "the coming of our Lord Jesus Christ with all his holy ones. [Amen.]" For Paul, spiritual development resulted in a more intense love of close neighbors and a more extensive love that included the whole human family. God's grace is an unlimited resource for strengthening our hearts and expanding our root capacity to grow in spiritual wisdom and overflowing love. The Apostle goes on to urgently exhort the Thessalonians to do even more to walk the path of righteousness charted by Christ, so that they will be judged blameless when the Lord returns (1 Thess 3:12—4:2).

Today, we can hear this passage as a compelling call to avoid settling for spiritual mediocrity, for halfhearted Christian discipleship, for a moral minimalism, and for a superficial understanding of our Christian faith. On the contrary, our vocation is to strive continually for greater spiritual maturity, a more wholehearted commitment to Christ, a life of more generous love, and a deeper understanding of the Christian tradition.

The spiritual masters suggest that we prayerfully discern the most effective next step we could take on our spiritual journey. A harried mother of three could adopt a simple daily exercise routine at home that would reduce her stress and increase her energy level. An executive who has trouble controlling his temper at work could attend a company-sponsored seminar on anger management. A social worker suffering from compassion fatigue could meditate regularly on the way Jesus responded to those in need. A father who feels inadequate in religious discussions initiated by his college-age daughter could read a book she finds interesting and discuss it with her. A cradle Catholic who has been satisfied with getting to Mass every Sunday could become more involved in the parish by serving on the social justice committee. An elderly nun who is no longer active in social ministry could follow the daily news and pick a person or cause to pray for that day.

What specific step could I take to cooperate with God's grace calling me to continued spiritual progress?

7. FOLLOWING OUR OWN UNIQUE PATH TO HOLINESS

Pope Francis has frequently reminded us that we are all called to holiness and that we may follow our own unique path to greater spiritual maturity. The Apostle Paul speaks to this point in 1 Corinthians 7:32–35, where he responds to a series of questions about sex and marriage sent to him by the newly established Christian community in Corinth. The questions arose in the context of the expectation that Christ would return soon to complete his mission. Does it make sense to get married? Should we stay married? Should we be celibate?

Paul's response is this: "I should like you to be free of anxieties," whether you are married or not. Married couples can be overly anxious about pleasing one another and caring for their families. Single people can be overly anxious about the things of the world. Paul, who was not married, does not want to lay down any specific directions about marriage and celibacy, but he does want everyone to adhere "to the Lord without distraction."

Although our contemporary worldview is so different from mid-first-century Corinthians, we can still find wisdom in Paul's response. Excessive anxiety in any situation can be debilitating. Adherence to the Lord, trust in God, and reliance on the Holy Spirit can help us manage our anxieties. A young man, married for four years with two children and now suffering from doubts about his choice of a spouse, would do well to put his full energy into being a good husband and a loving father, while praying for strength and guidance in meeting his responsibilities. Periodic self-examination is an important practice for spiritual growth. On the other hand, excessive introspection can be paralyzing, especially when directed to fundamental vocation choices.

Paul's response also suggests that any state of life can serve as a path to holiness. As Vatican II emphasized, there are no second-class members of the Church. By virtue of our baptism, we are all called to live a holy life and to do our part to spread the reign of God in the world. Married couples have their own distinctive ways of growing spiritually as couples and individually. They can share spiritual exercises: participating in Sunday liturgy, praying before meals and before going to bed, reading and reflecting on scripture, participating in a Marriage Encounter, and attending a retreat. They can work together to deepen their understanding of their faith: attending a parish lecture series, reading a theological book, and watching educational programs on television. They can also think in terms of helping their partner grow as a person. For example, a wife could encourage her overweight husband to exercise regularly and eat properly; a husband could encourage his nonpracticing wife to start attending Mass with him again.

Single persons, whether by choice or circumstances, can find many ways to lead a holy communal life by cultivating healthy friendships, helping to humanize their workplace, contributing to the life of their parish, and participating in civic life. They can also follow their own unique personal path to holiness by developing a prayer regimen that fits their own rhythm of life, adopting a meditation technique that touches their heart, or finding a spiritual director who understands their unique journey. All states of life provide opportunities to grow in holiness.

What next concrete step could I take to become a holier person?

8. SEEING OTHERS AS CHILDREN OF GOD

In a world where so many people are treated as non-persons, less than human, disposable objects, we Christians need to stand up for the fundamental dignity and worth of every human being. First John 3:1–2 expresses a powerful truth when the unknown author, a follower of the Beloved Disciple, declares, "See what love the Father has bestowed on us that we may be called the children of God." God's love for us is generative, creating an intimate relationship with us, deeper and stronger than the relationship between good fathers and their offspring. We are not just *called* children of God; we truly *are* children of God. This is our fundamental being, our most important reality, our most precious gift. This blessing is not earned or deserved. It is freely given by our God who is generous beyond measure. As we walk this earth, we are already God's children, but the fullness of that reality will be achieved and recognized only when we see God face-to-face in heaven.

The author warns us that the world does not "know us," suggesting that there are those who do not understand, accept, or live this intimate relationship between God and the human family. We cannot speak glibly of our status as children of God, because there is so much counterevidence in our world today. Large numbers of people commit suicide every year. Human beings are still bought and sold in active slave trading. Young girls are caught up in the sex industry. The clergy sex abuse scandal has revealed the horrible wounds inflicted on innocent young people. Domestic violence is all too common. Millions of refugees roam the earth, displaced from their homes. Bullying of young people causes great emotional harm. School shootings take innocent lives. More abuses of women by powerful men are coming to light.

This massive assault on human dignity causes some to doubt the existence of a loving God. The claim that we are children of God is not self-evident. It is a faith statement that flies in the face of our expanding knowledge of evil made possible by modern media. The true depth of our intimate relationship with God remains mysterious to us, beyond our comprehension, exceeding the limited range of our imagination. It is possible to miss the moral imperative implied in our familial relationship to God, for example, our obligation to treat others as brothers and sisters and our responsibility to care for the most vulnerable of God's children.

We can all benefit from prayerful reflection on our status as children of God, remembering troubled students who lack self-confidence, depressed individuals tempted to suicide, women being taken advantage of by men, gay persons coping with a homophobic culture, elderly persons who are feeling worthless, public servants recognizing they are underappreciated, single women striving to overcome negative stereotypes, comfortable believers inoculated against the sufferings of the less fortunate, former believers overwhelmed by the pain endured by innocent victims, doubtful believers who wonder if God has forgotten his children, and Christians who need a reminder that we are called to active love for our sisters and brothers in God's family.

How does being a child of God impact my fundamental attitude?

9. OVERCOMING SPIRITUAL COMPLACENCY

We all know something of the temptation to settle for mediocrity in our spiritual life, to be satisfied with our limited understanding and practice of the faith. The Letter to the Ephesians, one of the most influential of the New Testament letters on Christian spirituality, challenges various forms of spiritual complacency. Traditionally attributed to the Apostle Paul, most contemporary scholars think Ephesians was written in the 90s by one of the great interpreters of Paul, who understood the spiritual significance of the Apostle's teaching.

In chapter 5, the author uses the metaphor of moving from darkness to light to describe the transformation demanded of Christian disciples: "You were once darkness, but now you are light in the Lord. Live as children of light" who practice moral virtues, share in God's righteousness, and act sincerely without pretense. The passage goes on to enjoin us to expose the works of darkness, presumably by good example that brings to light shameful behavior done in secret. It ends with another admonition: "Awake, O sleeper, and arise from the dead, and Christ will give you light" (Eph 5:8–14).

We can hear this passage as a call to conversion to greater spiritual growth. We must stay awake and keep a clear eye so we can pass from the darkness of sin to the light of virtue, and the benign neglect of evil to an effort to expose and overcome social sin. Enlightened by Christ, we should pursue moral goodness, participate in God's righteousness, and strive to live with authentic honesty. These imperatives of the epistle can be reinforced by the gospel story of Christ's cure of the man blind from birth, who becomes progressively more aware of the Lord's identity, while the Pharisees, upset at Jesus for healing on the Sabbath, become progressively more blind to the truth (see John 9:1–41).

It is not hard to envision Christians making spiritual progress as suggested by Ephesians. A middle-aged bachelor who lived a life of selfish hedonism got serious about his Christian upbringing and began helping people in need and serving his community. A woman, who for years tolerated a "soft" racism in her social circle, cultivated a friendship with a black female parishioner. A college student who recognized the inadequacy of his grade school knowledge of his Catholic faith took an elective theology course as part of a sincere effort to gain a more mature understanding of his faith.

How can I live more authentically as a child of the light?

10. TRUSTING IN GOD'S MERCY

As we try to remember that we cannot earn our way into heaven by good works, we find reinforcement in Ephesians 2:4–10, which emphasizes God's merciful love for us manifested in our intimate union with Christ. "Even when we were dead in our transgressions," God "brought us to life with Christ," "raised us up with him, and seated us with him in the heavens." Our salvation is already accomplished. As we walk this earth, we already share in the death, resurrection, and glorification of Christ. This great gift is not due to us by virtue of our good works but is received as an unmerited gift of God, showing "the immeasurable riches of his grace." Although we already share in Christ's saving work, we still await the final definitive victory of God's merciful love. We are already God's "handiwork," created anew in Christ, but we are called to continue to grow closer to the Lord and to share more completely by "good works" in his mission to save the world.

The passage offers important points worth consideration today. It explicitly warns us against boasting about our good works. We cannot claim before God that we have earned salvation by our exemplary behavior. As the epistle puts it, "For by grace you have been saved through faith." Salvation is free, a gift of God beyond anything we could possibly merit or earn. The proper response is gratitude, not pride of accomplishment. A Catholic accountant who is proud that his spiritual ledger shows far more virtue than vice could respond to the passage by relying less on his good works and more on God's mercy as the only true source of salvation.

A healthy emphasis on God's unconditional love and immeasurable mercy is good news for those who suffer from various forms of spiritual anxiety: fear of damnation, unrealistic guilt feelings, excessive worry about mortal sins, inability to accept divine forgiveness. The epistle suggests a radical solution to all such negative feelings: trust in God's mercy rather than our own accomplishments. It helps to spend more time cultivating our intimate relationship with Christ and less time worrying about sins and failures. Ann, a cradle Catholic happily married with three adult children (two still practicing Catholics) and six grandchildren (one with serious emotional problems), lived her whole life with a legalistic outlook on her Catholic faith. In her late fifties, she took a course in contemporary theology that proved to be life transforming. She came to see her Catholic faith not as a series of demanding rules but as a liberating commitment to Christ. Over time, her new theological insights touched her heart, enabling her to put greater trust in God while worrying less about possible sins. This freed her for a more joyful approach to life and improved relationships with family and friends. When Ann reflects on the passage from Ephesians, she has an intuitive appreciation of its fundamental meaning and importance.

How can I trust more in God's mercy and less in my own accomplishments?

11. TRUSTING IN GOD'S PROMISES

Hebrews 11 identifies faith as the key to trusting the divine promises. The passage begins with the often quoted verse: "Faith is the realization of what is hoped for and evidence of things not seen." The precise meaning of this verse is not immediately clear. It is not intended as a nuanced theological explanation of faith. It is more poetic and evocative, suggesting what faith does and how it functions. People of faith trust that what they hope for will happen, that God will keep the divine promise of salvation. It is rooted in the firm conviction that God is trustworthy, that God's love is unconditional, and that God's promises are irrevocable.

The unknown author of Hebrews makes his abstract description of faith more concrete by raising the biblical figure of Abraham as a real-life example of a living faith. The story begins with Abraham following God's call to leave his homeland and sojourn in a foreign land. Abraham not only demonstrated his faith by heading for an unknown destination; he also trusted God's promise that a seventy-six-year-old man with a sterile wife would produce numerous descendants, a promise that seemed doomed when Abraham was prepared to follow God's command to sacrifice his son, Isaac.

Reflection on Abraham's faith draws attention to the way God's promises have continued to be fulfilled throughout history. As Christians, we believe God kept his promise to be present to his people by sending his Son to dwell in our midst. God made irrevocable his promise to save the whole human family by raising the crucified Jesus to life and sending the Holy Spirit to guide and unify us.

This reflection on faith brings to my mind Catholic parents who learned to trust God's promise as they dealt with the tragic death of their beloved and gifted eighteen-year-old son in an automobile accident. Their immediate and instinctive anger at God for taking their son quickly gave way to prayers for God's strength and guidance. They knew an initial temptation to seek revenge against the drunken driver who caused them unspeakable anguish, but eventually they came to forgive him. They were amazed and comforted by so many of their son's classmates and friends who spoke so highly of him and the good he did in his brief life. The parents helped plan the funeral liturgy and distributed communion at the Mass. During their grieving process after the burial, they put extra effort into caring for their other four children. They established a scholarship in their son's memory at his Catholic high school. Aware that such tragedies sometimes split parents and lead to divorce, they wisely worked on supporting one another, sharing their emotional struggles, and praying together for guidance. Over time, they found a measure of comfort in their belief that their son now lives with God, where all his youthful dreams are completely fulfilled. Looking back on the whole heartbreaking experience, the parents agree that it has, in ways mysterious, strengthened their faith. We can say they know by experience the truth of today's epistle that God is trustworthy, and we can count on the divine promise to sustain us on our journey, even in the worst of times.

How has my faith enabled me to remain hopeful?

12. USING OUR GIFTS TO BUILD UP THE BODY OF CHRIST

We have all received unmerited gifts of the Holy Spirit that can be used for selfish purposes or for the common good. The Apostle Paul deals with this issue in 1 Corinthians 12:3–13, which concentrates on various manifestations of the Spirit in the gifts, ministries, and works of the Christian community. It seems there were some disputes among the Corinthian Christians about the character, prominence, and function of some of the gifts. Attempting to heal these divisions in the church he founded, Paul writes, "There are different kinds of spiritual gifts but the same Spirit." He goes on, "To each individual the manifestation of the Spirit is given for some benefit," suggesting all the various gifts, ministries, and works are not for personal gain but for the good of the whole community. The Apostle then indicates that the Church, which is the Body of Christ, should function harmoniously, like the human body, which has many parts all working together as one body. He concludes, "For in one Spirit we were all baptized into one body, whether Jews or Greeks, slaves or free persons, and we were all given to drink of one Spirit."

As Christians initiated into the life of the Church, we all have received gifts of the Holy Spirit. They are not earned or merited, nor should they be a source of pride or personal reward. On the contrary, we should be grateful for them, develop them as best we can, and use them to serve the good of the community. With respect for the unique gifts and roles of others, we should look for ways to cooperate in the great work of building up the Body of Christ and spreading the reign of God in the world.

Eyes of faith can detect the Holy Spirit at work among members of vibrant parishes today: religious educators who use their knowledge of theology to help parishioners, young and old, to gain a deeper understanding of their faith; deacons who lead the effort to serve the needs of the poor in their parishes and the surrounding neighborhood; members of parish councils who provide good leadership because they care about the parish and spend time understanding the desires and needs of the various segments of the congregation; music ministers who engage the assembly in lively, theologically sound, and liturgically appropriate singing at Mass; parishioners who provide free meals after funeral Masses for those who are grieving the loss of loved ones; liturgical ministers who pray regularly to meet their responsibilities to greet the people, proclaim the scriptures, and distribute communion at Mass; co-chairs of the pro-life and the social justice committees who meet periodically to make sure they are contributing to the good of the parish; members of the finance committee who use their expertise to help the parish remain solvent and use resources wisely in carrying out the parish mission; the secretaries who use their interpersonal skills to create a welcoming atmosphere for visitors as well as regular parishioners; pastoral administrators who use their practical know-how to keep the parish running smoothly; parishioners who contribute financially to support the parish; pastors who identify the talents of their parishioners, help develop them, and coordinate them for the good of the parish.

How can I better use my gifts to enhance the life of my parish?

13. RESPONDING TO THE HOLY SPIRIT

The spirituality of many Western Catholics centers on the Father and his son Jesus Christ, leaving little room for the role of the Holy Spirit, who plays a greater role in Eastern Christianity. The New Testament encourages us to be more engaged with the Holy Spirit. For example, Acts 2:1–11 puts great emphasis on the Holy Spirit descending on the apostles on the Jewish Feast of Pentecost in the form of "tongues as of fire," and John 20:19–23 tells us that Jesus breathed the Holy Spirit on the disciples on Easter Sunday evening.

In 1 Corinthians 12:3–13, Paul identifies a fundamental function of the Holy Spirit: "No one can say, 'Jesus is Lord' except by the holy Spirit." Our English word *Lord* translates the Greek word *kyrios*, which was used for God in the Greek translation of the Hebrew Scriptures and was commonly used as the official title of the Roman emperor. In other words, the Holy Spirit enables us to recognize Jesus as sharing the divine nature and reminds us that he is our true King above any earthly ruler.

Paul goes on to describe the role of the Holy Spirit as the source of the unity in diversity that characterizes the Christian community at its best. There are different kinds of spiritual gifts, such as speaking in tongues and prophesying, but also gifts for those performing tasks, such as serving at table and attending to finances. All the gifts of the Spirit are given not for personal benefit but for the common good.

To explain his notion of unity in diversity found in the ideal Christian community, Paul uses the image of the human body, which is "one though it has many parts, and all the parts of the body, though many, are one body." This metaphor suggests that the Christian community should celebrate individual contributions that promote the common good and should foster constructive cooperation that avoids a dull uniformity and destructive competition. The passage concludes, "For in one Spirit we were all baptized into one body, whether Jews or Greeks, slaves or free persons, and we were all given to drink of one Spirit."

We can hear this passage as an invitation to be more attentive to the prompting of the Holy Spirit, who gives all the baptized special gifts to build up the Body of Christ. An authoritarian pastor could become far more effective by functioning as a servant leader charged with identifying, encouraging, and coordinating the gifts and talents of his parishioners. A parish social justice committee could gain new energy by adding some social activists to their more moderate membership. An all-male parish finance council could become more productive by adding women to the group. A parish could improve its liturgies by consulting with a liturgical expert.

How could I be more responsive to the promptings of the Holy Spirit?

14. SHARING OUR FAITH

As we take seriously our responsibility to share our Christian faith, we can take the Apostle Paul as a wise guide. Paul founded the church in Corinth around AD 51 on his second missionary journey and lived there for about a year and a half. A few years later while in Ephesus during his third missionary journey, Paul received word that various troubles had befallen the community, including a divisive factionalism. Seeing himself as a father to the community, Paul wrote his first letter to the Corinthian church, instructing them in the fundamentals of their faith and encouraging them to overcome their divisions.

Following the common pattern of Greek letters, Paul first introduces himself as "an apostle of Christ Jesus by the will of God." Although he did not interact with Jesus during his public life, he did encounter the risen Christ, who commissioned him to preach the gospel to the Gentiles, according to the "the will of God." The Apostle to the Gentiles addresses his letter to the church in Corinth, a community "sanctified in Christ" and "called to be holy." Paul reminds the Corinthians that they are united with the larger community of "all those everywhere who call upon the name of our Lord Jesus Christ, their Lord and ours." Paul concludes his greeting, "Grace to you and peace from God the Father and the Lord Jesus Christ" (1 Cor 1:1–3).

The epistle reminds us of the decisive importance of Paul in the spread of the Christian faith around the world. He found a way to implant the fundamental message of Jesus (a Jew who spoke Aramaic and generally confined his mission to the house of Israel) in the Gentile world where it grew organically. For example, Paul took the kingdom language of Jesus, rooted in the Hebrew Scriptures, and transposed it into language about the life-giving Spirit unleashed by the death and resurrection of Christ. Like Paul, we can think of ourselves as apostles sent by the Lord to implant the gospel message in our own setting: for example, a mother transforms her home into a domestic church, a manager creates a worksite where employees are encouraged to develop their talents, a teacher makes the classroom a fun place to learn, a coach creates an environment where athletes learn sportsmanship, a domestic judge runs a courtroom that favors reform and reconciliation, and a pastor develops a parish that fosters spiritual growth.

How can I share my faith in my sphere of influence?

15. USING OUR GIFTS TO ENHANCE PARISH LIFE

As parishes try to use their parishioners' talents to create more vibrant Christian communities, it is helpful to recall the Apostle Paul's advice in 1 Corinthians 12:4–11. In this passage, the Apostle insists that the various free gifts, or charisms, given to individuals in the community are all from the same Spirit and should be used not to divide the community but to enrich it. "There are different kinds of spiritual gifts but the same Spirit...Lord...[and] God." Paul then goes on to name the various gifts of the Spirit: wisdom, knowledge, faith, healing power, mighty deeds, prophecy, discernment, and speaking in tongues and interpreting their meaning. All these are given for the common good to benefit the community. Some, like prophecy, were exercised during the liturgy. Others, like attending to financial matters, were more mundane but were necessary for the good order in the community. Still others, like wondrous healings, reminded the community of the enormous power of the Spirit.

It seems that some Corinthians who were blessed with great gifts adopted an attitude of superiority toward others in the community. This was especially true for those with the gift of tongues, who felt spiritually superior because they could speak in foreign languages or in ecstatic utterances that needed an interpreter to reveal their meaning and significance for the community. The tendency of the Corinthians to compare the spiritual gifts enjoyed by individuals led to pride and envy that contributed to the serious divisions plaguing the community. Paul responded to this problem by noting that all the gifts were bestowed and sustained by the Holy Spirit, and by insisting that they all were given not for personal advantage but for the benefit of the whole community.

Today, the Holy Spirit continues to bless individuals with gifts to build up the Body of Christ and spread the kingdom in the world. Much of this Spirit-inspired activity goes on in parishes where the Church is actualized. Following the directives of Vatican II, effective pastors identify gifted individuals, encourage their development, and coordinate their contributions to the parish. Since Vatican II ended in 1965, we have seen a remarkable transformation of parish life from priests doing almost all the ministry to parishioners contributing their gifts and talents to the parish and its mission. Talented musicians provide appropriate music for Mass. Dedicated eucharistic ministers take communion to the sick, visiting and praying with them. Individuals with leadership skills serve on parish councils. Married couples share their experience with engaged couples. Activists familiar with

Catholic social teaching lead social justice committees. Secretaries with good social skills make parishioners and visitors feel welcome. Catechists with degrees in theology run religious education programs for adults and their children. In these and more hidden ways, parishioners, empowered by the Holy Spirit, are using their gifts to enrich parish life.

How can I best use my gifts to serve my parish?

16. FACING THE FUTURE WITH TRUST IN GOD

Achieving a healthy attitude toward the future is not easy, given the temptations to ignore it, control it, and obsess over it. Second Peter, written by an anonymous author representing the tradition of Peter, perhaps as late as AD 130, deals with the future, specifically the day of the Lord, the promised and expected second coming of Christ, now delayed for almost a century. The author argues that God's timing is not ours: "With the Lord one day is like a thousand years and a thousand years like one day." Thus he can say, "The Lord does not delay his promise." What we experience as delay is really an expression of the patience of God, who does not wish "that any should perish but that all should come to repentance." In other words, the "delay" is to our benefit, providing an opportunity for repentance. It remains true, however, that the day of the Lord will come, "like a thief," at an unknown hour. Therefore, it is vital that we stay alert, conducting ourselves in "holiness and devotion," living "without spot or blemish," and peacefully awaiting "new heavens and a new earth in which righteousness dwells" (2 Pet 8–16).

Although most Christians today are not terribly distressed by the delayed day of the Lord, we all live in the time between Christ's life on this earth and the fulfillment of his promise to return and complete his mission. We all face an unknown future, waiting for what lies ahead. It is possible to mismanage the future in various ways: failing to prepare properly for future possibilities (not saving for retirement), attempting to control an uncontrollable future (forcing children to follow an unwise career path), giving in to cynicism about creating a better future (withdrawing from the electoral process), fretting excessively about remote negative possibilities (being abducted by a drug cartel).

The epistle suggests a Christian outlook on the future that we might call "active patience" or "patient activity." This virtue is based on trust in God, who is faithful to the divine promises, who accompanies us on our journey, and who assures us of the final victory of good over evil. It inclines persons to wait patiently, to accept calmly the unknowable future, and to prepare prudently for contingencies. This virtue flourishes when we follow the advice of the epistle by striving for holiness that trusts God and developing a healthy devotional life that fosters an integrated spirituality.

We can find inspiration in the persons who practice active patience. A widow managed her nightly bout of anxiety over the salvation of her soul by saying the rosary for one of her relatives in need. A collegian used his fear of rejection for grad school as a catalyst for studying harder and earning better grades. A citizen distressed by political polarization rose above cynicism by getting involved in the campaign of a candidate she trusted. A sister who felt overwhelmed by the evil in our world prayed for the gift of hope, which helped her recognize positive trends in our society. A mother persevered for years in tough love and daily prayers for her alcoholic son, always hopeful that he would eventually manage his disease with God's help.

How could I cope better with my unknown future?

17. MAINTAINING HOPE

As we deal with the never-ending, sometimes heavy trials of everyday life, we need to keep hope alive so that we do not get overwhelmed and feel like giving up. We can find encouragement in 1 Peter 1:3–9, which grounds hope in fundamental Christian truths. The passage begins with praise for God the Father who, "in his great mercy," gave us "a living hope" through the resurrection of Jesus from the dead, which prepared for us a heavenly inheritance "that is imperishable, undefiled, and unfading " to be fully "revealed in the final time." This sentence is long and complex but makes the essential point that God has prepared a heavenly reward for us through the death and resurrection of Jesus Christ.

The author goes on to put the "various trials" of his readers in perspective, probably problems of living their faith in a pagan environment. These trials may test the genuineness of their faith, like gold "tested by fire," but they can rejoice because one day they will share in "the praise, glory, and honor" of the risen Christ. The advice seems to be to put up with the trials of life for a little while for the sake of a much greater reward later. The passage ends by noting that those who have not seen Christ can still love and believe in him, rejoicing in his gift of eternal salvation. We can recall the encounter between doubting Thomas and the risen Lord, who says, "Blessed are those who have not seen and have believed" (John 20:19–31).

This passage is a rich resource for Christians who take time to reflect on it, seeking to grow in their faith. A grandfather who never got beyond a grade school knowledge of his faith could develop a more mature understanding of the role of Christ's resurrection in saving his soul. A wife with a good marriage but who is somewhat resentful that her husband does not do his share of domestic chores could decide to gracefully accept this limitation for the sake of future rewards in this life and the next. A husband who habitually put his career before his wife could ask forgiveness from the merciful God and work diligently to improve his marriage.

In what specific ways can trusting God help me grow spiritually?

18. MANAGING HARDSHIPS

We all know something of the hardships of life: physical ailments, emotional distress, financial setbacks, toilsome work, and spiritual aridity. Faced with our own personal hardships, let us turn to 2 Timothy, which was traditionally attributed to Paul but was probably written by one of his disciples in the late first century. The letter is cast in the form of a last farewell from Paul in prison offering encouragement to his disciple Timothy to bear the hardships entailed in preaching the gospel and in living it daily. It teaches the fundamental truth that God saves all of us not by our own works but "according to his own design." In the divine plan, God's grace comes to us "in Christ Jesus before time began, but now made manifest through the appearance of our savior Christ Jesus, who destroyed death and brought life and immortality to light through the gospel" (1:8–10). In other words, Christ, the Word with God from all eternity, became human in our history and by his death and resurrection won for us the pure gift of eternal life with God. As part of the plan, Christ calls all of us to a life of holiness inspired by the gospel.

This teaching is consistent with familiar gospel stories. For example, Matthew's story of the transfiguration of Jesus has God proclaim to Peter, James, and John, "This is my beloved Son, with whom I am well pleased; listen to him"

(Matt 17:5). Once again, this encounter comes as a pure gift to very unworthy disciples in need of strength as they face the crosses of discipleship.

We can imagine individuals better managing their hardships by reflecting on this passage. A cradle Catholic who spent many years accumulating merits as a down payment on heaven came to see salvation as an unearned gift from God that freed him to be more grateful and less worried about possible damnation. A former drug addict who kicked the habit by turning her life over to Jesus embarked on a more fruitful spiritual journey when she heard the Lord calling her not just to avoid drugs but to live a life of holiness. A social activist greatly discouraged by continuing racial tensions vowed to continue his efforts after pondering the Pauline assurance that God gives us strength to carry out our Christian responsibilities.

Do I appreciate the free gift of salvation won by Christ for me?

19. GETTING MORE OUT OF LENT

The season of Lent provides great opportunities for spiritual growth. If we need encouragement to seize these opportunities, we can reflect on the crucial eighth chapter of Paul's letter to the Romans (8:31–34). Through some pointed rhetorical questions that emphasize God's superabundant love for us in Christ, the Apostle offers a powerful message of hope to the Christian community already existing in Rome. "If God is for us, who can be against us?" Recalling that God handed over his own Son for all of us, Paul asks, "How will he not also give us everything else with him?" Evoking the image of a courtroom, he asks, with God on our side, who will bring a charge against us and who will condemn us?

Paul continues with the reminder that Christ Jesus, crucified and risen, is at the right hand of God, interceding for us.

As we move through the Lenten season, this passage encourages us to persevere in carrying the crosses of everyday life as well as the self-imposed crosses of voluntary penance. God is for us, always on our side in the great struggle against the dark forces. Christ continues to intercede for us as we strive to do good and grow spiritually. We are God's chosen ones, acquitted of sin and strengthened by grace to spread the reign of justice and peace in the world.

We can imagine individuals who could benefit from an encouraging word about Lent. A nominal Catholic who usually skips Sunday Mass during Lent could decide to attend each week, hoping for strength to manage his stressful job. A woman who fasted during the first week of Lent without losing any weight, could persevere in her effort to develop better eating habits, trusting that something good will come of it. A young man who has already failed twice in his Lenten resolution to avoid pornography could resolve to persevere in his efforts to develop a healthy outlook on sexuality. A veteran peace activist, feeling discouraged and depleted, could use Lent as a retreat to revive her hope, to reenergize her spirit, and to recommit herself to the cause.

What motivates me to persevere in my Lenten practices?

20. LIVING OUR BAPTISMAL PRIESTHOOD

Among Catholics in the United States, we are still trying to work out healthy relationships between clergy and laity. Colossians 2:12–14 can help us in this important issue. The passage begins, "You were buried with him in baptism, in which you were also raised with him through faith in the power of God, who raised him from the dead." The passage goes on to indicate that through baptism God brings us to life along with Christ, forgives all our transgressions, and obliterates "the bond against us," a legal notion referring to a debt due to sin.

We can use this passage as a springboard for further reflection on the sacrament of baptism. The Second Vatican Council (1962–65) taught that through baptism we are incorporated into the people of God and reborn as sons and daughters of God, with responsibilities to worship our Creator and to spread and defend our faith. All baptized Christians share in the universal priesthood of Christ and his saving ministry. By virtue of baptism, and not merely by hierarchical delegation, all the faithful are co-responsible for building up the Body of Christ and for spreading the reign of God in the world. All Christians, and not just clergy, are called to holiness and to greater spiritual maturity. All the baptized find nourishment and guidance through full, active, and conscious participation in the eucharistic liturgy.

Today most Catholic parishes employ the Rite of Christian Initiation for Adults (RCIA) to prepare adult converts for baptism at the Easter Vigil. This development, fostered by Vatican II, makes it clear that baptism finds its fullest meaning as a ritual expression of an adult commitment to share in the priesthood of Christ as a member of the Church.

A growing number of Catholics are taking seriously their vocation to practice their baptismal priesthood. Many meet this responsibility by actively contributing to the life of their parish, for example, participating in the liturgy as eucharistic ministers and lectors and contributing their talents to various organizations, such as pastoral councils and social justice committees. Others live out their baptismal priesthood by helping to extend the kingdom in their circle of influence: parents establishing and maintaining loving families, public officials promoting the common good, employers humanizing their worksites, compassionate persons performing the works of mercy, coaches teaching teamwork to their players, teachers enabling their students to become lifelong learners, social workers helping persons manage their own lives, and all those who make the world a better place by doing justice, loving the good, and walking humbly.

How could I exercise my baptismal priesthood more effectively?

21. COOPERATING WITH GOD'S GRACE

It is not always easy to maintain a proper relationship or fruitful interaction between the fundamental Christian doctrine that we are totally dependent on God's grace for spiritual growth and ultimate salvation, and our personal responsibility to do everything we can to cooperate with divine grace on our spiritual journey. In working out this relationship, we can find helpful guidance in the spiritually rich eighth chapter of Paul's long letter to the Romans (8:28–39). The Apostle begins by addressing his brothers and sisters: "We know that all things work for good for those who love God, who are called according to his purpose." From all eternity God has had a plan to bring the evolving created world to its final fulfillment and to save all people. The divine plan does not eliminate all evil and suffering, but it does work for our benefit by bringing good out of bad situations. God saves us by conforming us "to the image of his Son, so that he might be the firstborn among many brothers [and sisters]." Salvation is open to all through the death and resurrection of Christ.

Paul goes on to explain the dynamics of the divine plan. From all eternity God foreknew and predestined those to be saved. "And those he predestined he also called; and those he called he also justified; and those he justified he also glorified."

This succinct summary of God's saving activity is difficult to understand and has generated diverse theological positions. At one extreme is the influential Protestant theologian John Calvin (1509–64), who held a double predestination, meaning God predestined some to be saved and others to be damned. This view made it hard to defend human freedom and triggered speculation about who was saved and on what criteria. In 1547, the Council of Trent condemned Calvin's position, insisting that our salvation is totally dependent on God's gratuitous gift of grace but also requires our free response. Due to the teachings of Vatican II, Catholics have developed a more optimistic attitude toward salvation. God does not predestine anyone to hell but wills the salvation of all people. As Pope Francis insists, God is merciful to us, never tiring of extending forgiveness to all human beings. This good news does not absolve us from doing our part, from cooperating with divine grace, from striving to do God's will, from seeking forgiveness, and from a systematic effort to grow spiritually. We can find a balanced approach in St. Augustine's aphorism: Pray like everything depends on God; work like everything depends on you.

Let us imagine individuals who could benefit from reflection on this passage. A woman suffering from MS could come to realize that her illness has made her more compassionate. A collegian with low self-esteem could begin to build greater self-confidence by realizing God wants him to flourish. A religion teacher could be moved to read more on the salvation optimism taught by Vatican II. A successful executive who is excessively proud of her accomplishments could become more appreciative of her many undeserved blessings received from God. A grandfather who is overly fearful of going to hell could find some comfort by reflecting regularly on God's mercy. A homemaker might manage her demanding life more effectively by saying brief prayers throughout the day and by recognizing the importance of her domestic responsibilities.

What adjustments must I make to achieve a more balanced spirituality?

22. APPROPRIATING THE FUNDAMENTAL TRUTH THAT GOD IS LOVE

Our Christian tradition insists that God is incomprehensible, beyond all our images and thoughts. And yet there is also a long tradition of naming God, of finding helpful images of the Deity, of refining our language about God. As Christian believers, we are called to deepen and refine our image of God. In this ongoing process we do well to reflect on 1 John 4:7–10, an inspiring and insightful meditation on Christian love. It begins, "Beloved, let us love one another, because love is of God." The author then tells us that loving others is what enables us to know God, "for God is love." God has revealed the depth of divine love by sending "his only Son into the world so that we might have life through him." The passage concludes with a reminder of the true origin of love: "not that we have loved God, but that he loved us and sent his Son as expiation for our sins."

There are many ways of imaging God: the man upstairs who is in charge, the divine Santa Claus who rewards good people, the benign observer who created the world and lets it run its course, the strict bookkeeper who keeps track of our good deeds as well as our sins, the sober judge who will decide our ultimate fate, and many more. By declaring "God is love," the epistle gives us a more profound and endearing notion of the Deity. God is the Source and Goal of the love that energizes and guides the human adventure. God is our loving Father, who is more compassionate and caring than the best of human fathers. Divine love is overflowing, abundant, creative, effective, alluring, inexhaustible, and ultimately mysterious, beyond comprehension.

God's love is most fully revealed to us in the incarnation, the Word becoming flesh, the Son of God living in our midst. Christ's life of self-sacrificing love, even to death on the cross, indicates the compassionate character of divine love—God suffering with us.

Through God's love for us, we are created in the divine image and established as brothers and sisters in God's family. As the Eastern fathers emphasized, we are divinized, transformed by grace, constituted as temples of the Holy Spirit. We did not earn this love, nor do we deserve it. It comes, rather, as a gratuitous gift from the God who first loved us. This gift of love carries a moral obligation to share it with others by our own concrete acts of compassionate service. It is in loving our neighbor that we come to know in a deeper way that God is love.

We can imagine individuals benefiting from this meditation on love. A woman plagued by excessive guilt could find greater peace by seeing God less as a severe judge and more as a loving Father. A self-centered man who exploited others for his own benefit could learn to treat others with genuine love and respect. An engineer who practiced her Catholic faith mainly by keeping the rules could put more emphasis on living the law of love. A truck driver who is overly proud of his generous service to others could develop the virtue of humility by remembering God has first loved him, empowering him to love others.

How can my spiritual life be enriched by praying to the God who is love?

23. TRANSFORMING OUR AFFLICTIONS INTO SPIRITUAL GROWTH

Affliction and suffering are built into human life. As Christians, we look to our faith to help us manage all our crosses in life. In 2 Corinthians 4:13—5:1, the Apostle Paul reflects on the suffering he has experienced in his ministry. He is not discouraged, however, because he believes that the God who raised the crucified Jesus to life will also raise him and his Corinthian converts to life with Christ. Comparing his current suffering to his eternal reward, he insists "this momentary light affliction is producing for us an eternal weight of glory beyond all comparison." Paul invites us to keep perspective on our own suffering by paying more attention to our inner self that is being "renewed day by day" than to our outer self that is wasting away. He wants us to "look not to what is seen but to what is unseen." In other words, our faith makes it possible to transform suffering into spiritual growth and to turn obstacles into opportunities.

In applying Paul's teaching, it is important to avoid utopian thinking and glib talk. The monstrous suffering connected with the Gulag, the Holocaust, and the Killing Fields preclude easy answers. Parents grieving over the death of an only child may not be ready to hear talk of the happiness of heaven. Human suffering retains a mysterious quality that defies simple explanations.

Nevertheless, there are Christians who live the truth proclaimed by Paul in the epistle. There are believers who are not discouraged despite enduring many hardships. Some find a way to transform their afflictions into spiritual growth. Others gracefully bear their crosses, hopeful that they will share in the victory of the risen Christ. This reading makes me think of a former student of mine whom I will call Jill. She has known more than her share of suffering since completing college. Her marriage, which began with realistic positive expectations, has proven mediocre at best, and her teaching career has brought more disappointments than achievements. Her youngest daughter has struggled with drug addiction since her teenage years, and her son, who has done well in the corporate world, has distanced himself from the family. She herself has struggled with rheumatoid arthritis, which limits her mobility, and with periodic bouts of depression that can be controlled with medication. Since college, she has maintained contacts with a couple of good women friends who have been a source of comfort to her. Now in her sixties, she has continued to practice her Catholic faith. She goes to Mass regularly, participates in a prayer group, and meditates on a scripture passage most days.

Jill's faith has kept her from giving in to cynicism and frustration. She has learned to accept with a mostly calm heart her husband's emotional limitations. Grateful that her eldest daughter has turned out so well, she believes that her troubled younger daughter remains in God's tender embrace. Her motherly heart longs to reconnect with her son, moving her to say extra prayers for him. She thanks God every day for her college friends who have stayed in touch. In her prayer group, she avoids complaining about her life and tries to be attentive to the needs of the other members. Jill's story, simplified and disguised as it is, can remind us all of the power of faith to deal with the crosses that inevitably come our way.

Can I think of specific examples when my faith enabled me to carry on amid affliction?

24. HONORING THE HOLY SPIRIT

Historically, Western Christian spirituality has centered on God our Father and on Christ our Redeemer with much less attention paid to the Holy Spirit. Those interested in making the Spirit more a part of their spirituality can find guidance in Romans 8:14–17, which highlights the role of the Spirit in our relationship to our Creator and Redeemer. Compelled by the "Spirit of God," which later Christians identified as the Holy Spirit, the third person of the Trinity, we are truly children of God. Adopted into God's family, we can address God as "Abba," an Aramaic word used by children, like our *daddy*, and the word Jesus used to refer to his heavenly Father. Paul goes on to note that as children of God we are "joint heirs with Christ," which suggests that we already participate in Christ's divine life during our earthly journey and will do so more fully in the life of heaven. If we suffer with Christ, we will also "be glorified with him."

For most of us in the Western Christian world, Paul's emphasis on the role of the Holy Spirit can serve as a welcomed addition to our christocentric spirituality. The New Testament speaks about two missions initiated by God the Father: sending his Son into the world to share our life completely and to die and rise for our salvation, and sending the Holy Spirit, the Advocate promised by Jesus, to be our ongoing inspiration and guide. Reflection on these two missions eventually led the Church to formulate the doctrine of the Trinity in the fourth century. While Eastern Christianity placed a great deal of emphasis on the divinizing activity of the Spirit, Western theology and spirituality tended to stress the role of Christ in saving us from sin. Recognizing the limitations of this historical development, Pope John Paul II urged us to "breathe with both lungs," suggesting that we appropriate more of Eastern spirituality with its emphasis on the role of the Holy Spirit in the Christian life. For example, today's epistle reminds us that the Spirit creates intimate relationships with the Father and the Son, so that we can address the omnipotent God as Father and can count on the help of Christ our brother. The Spirit, who unites all human beings, encourages interfaith dialogue and collaboration among diverse religious groups. The Paraclete, who guides believers, calls us to develop our talents and gifts to serve others and promote the common good. The Holy Spirit, the inexhaustible source of energy, encourages us to be passionate about praising God and loving others.

We can imagine Christians who grow spiritually by being more responsive to the promptings of the Spirit. A faithful Catholic who regularly prays to Christ his Lord could come to see Christ more as his brother, worthy of imitation. A woman who developed strong anti-Muslim feelings after 9/11 could come to see that the Spirit is at work in the Islamic tradition and in faithful Muslims. A father who does not understand his daughter's participation in the Charismatic movement could come to appreciate the passion and enthusiasm she now has for her inherited faith. A conservative Catholic who still has trouble accepting the Vatican II liturgical changes could come to understand that the Church guided by the Spirit must always be reforming itself to meet the needs of a new age.

How could I be more responsive to the presence of the Holy Spirit in my life?

25. KEEPING THE CHRISTMAS SPIRIT ALIVE

As we search for creative ways to keep alive the joyful spirit of our annual celebration of Christmas, let us recall Luke's familiar Christmas story: a Roman census forces Joseph and his pregnant wife Mary to travel from Nazareth, their hometown, to Bethlehem, the city of David; with no room in the inn, Mary gives birth and lays Jesus in a manger; an angel announces the birth of the savior to shepherds, and a multitude of heavenly hosts praise God and proclaim peace on earth. Luke's beautiful story touches our imagination, gladdens our hearts, sparks thought, and contributes to the liturgical celebration of Christmas.

Titus 2:11–14 can help us to appreciate the significance of Luke's Christmas story. In the birth of Jesus, the grace of God has appeared in history as salvation for all people. The baby in the manger, the Word made flesh, grew to adulthood and gave himself for us, even to death on the cross, to deliver us from the dark forces of a godless world. Christ taught us to reject "worldly desires" and "to live temperately, justly, and devoutly in this age," while awaiting the glory of his final triumph over evil. His self-sacrificing love cleansed for himself "a people as his own, eager to do what is good."

Furthermore, Titus adds an ethical dimension to our celebration of Christmas. Belief in the incarnation should make a difference in the way we conduct ourselves daily. We can imagine individuals following the moral guidance of Titus. A man who ate and drank too much at several Christmas parties decided to live more "temperately," establishing a healthy diet and limiting his consumption of alcohol. An affluent widow who let slide the usual family contributions to charitable causes after her husband's death committed herself to living more "justly" by renewing and increasing financial support for the neglected charities. An engineer who for years paid little attention to spiritual matters vowed to live more "devoutly" by regular prayerful reflection on the Gospels.

How could I put the Christmas message into action in my own life?

26. REJOICING ALWAYS

A few months after the Apostle Paul evangelized the Thessalonians in the year 50, he sent them a letter, the earliest of the twenty-seven books in the New Testament. In 1 Thessalonians 5:16–24, Paul instructs us, "Rejoice always. Pray without ceasing. In all circumstances give thanks, for this is the will of God for you in Christ Jesus." He then adds the pointed directive, "Do not quench the Spirit" but "test everything; retain what is good." The passage concludes with a hopeful reminder that God is faithful to the divine promise of salvation.

What are we to make of Paul's admonition to rejoice always? It is important to determine what the word *joy* means in the Christian tradition. It is not the same as happiness, which depends on favorable external factors. On the contrary, joy is an inner disposition, a deep abiding sense of peace that results from knowing that God loves us unconditionally and from being in proper relationships with others. Directly sought, joy eludes us; it comes, rather, as a by-product of trust in God's compassionate love for us. The English author C. S. Lewis said he was "surprised by joy," suggesting it was an undeserved gift from God and an unexpected blessing.

Paul suggests a connection between rejoicing always and praying without ceasing. Prayer is a form of truth telling, which helps us develop and maintain proper relationships with God, others, nature, and ourselves. When tempted to quench the Spirit, "prayer opens our hearts to the Holy Spirit whose fruits include joy." As temples of the Holy Spirit, it is possible to retain a joyful heart even amid the crosses of life that sadden us. "Rejoice always" does not have to be a glib phrase easily ignored; it can be a catalyst for spiritual growth leading to a joy that passes all understanding (Phil 4:7).

In our own time, we are blessed with an inspiring, living example of a joyful spirit in Pope Francis. In his public appearances, the pope exudes joy as he leads prayers, gives talks, meets with the famous, and reaches out to those who are poor, ill, imprisoned, and marginalized. His ready smile and calm demeanor suggest an inner peace with God and himself. We know that he nourishes his soul with a daily regimen of prayer, scripture reading, meditation, and private devotions. His openness to dialogue and his calm response to critics suggest an integrated and joyful spiritual life.

The pope's inner joy finds expression in his teaching, including his major writings *The Joy of the Gospel* and *The Joy of Love*. For Francis, a Christian "who loves Christ is full of joy and radiates joy" and does not "look like someone who just came from a funeral." In a talk to young people, he said if we are close to Christ, "we will have joy in our hearts and a smile on our face." Recognizing that following Christ demands accepting the cross, Francis still contends that the authentic Christian life is "full of joy." Reflecting on the life and teaching of Pope Francis adds credibility to Paul's admonition to rejoice always.

Who do I know that exudes Christian joy?

27. LEARNING FROM PAUL OF TARSUS AND TERESA OF CALCUTTA

As we strive to maintain a positive attitude in these troubled times, the Apostle Paul insists, "Rejoice in the Lord always. I shall say it again: rejoice!" The Apostle goes on to say, "Have no anxiety at all," but offer prayers of petition and gratitude to God. As we reflect on this positive message, it is helpful to recall that Paul wrote it when he was languishing in a Roman prison, possibly facing death. Paul is no utopian dreamer urging superficial joy out of touch with reality. He grounds joy not in an optimistic assessment of life situations but in the presence of Christ. Christians can avoid anxiety because "the Lord is near" (Phil 4:4–7).

The crucified and risen Christ is present to us in multiple ways, playing "in ten thousand places," as the Jesuit poet Gerard Manley Hopkins vividly expressed it. Christ is present in our hearts through the animating power of the Holy Spirit; in the scriptures as the normative witness to his life and teachings; in other people, especially in the needy, as he taught; and, when we gather for the Eucharist, in the assembly, the Liturgy of the Word, and the consecrated bread and wine. Paul admonishes us to rejoice always because Christ is ever present, at the very center of our daily lives.

Mother Teresa, now the canonized saint of Calcutta, can serve as an instructive example of Christian joy that is authentic, realistic, and abiding. We recall that she left a happy home at the age of eighteen, joined the Sisters of Our Lady of Loreto, and taught in a Catholic high school in Calcutta for several years. On September 10, 1946, while traveling on a train, Christ called her "to go out in the streets to serve the poorest of the poor." She followed this vocation for five decades, always with a joyful smile on her face.

We now know, however, that she did so at a great price, without any further encouraging words from the Lord, without any sense of spiritual consolation. She felt abandoned by Christ, suffering "pain without ceasing" and "untold agony." She continued to speak publicly about "the tender love of God" and yet privately admitted to her spiritual director that "no light or inspiration enters my soul," leaving her with the "terrible pain of loss of God not wanting me." After a decade of such spiritual suffering, she took the advice of her spiritual director and came "to love the darkness," which brought her "a deep joy." For the rest of her life, the saint of Calcutta ministered to Christ present in the poorest of the poor, radiating inner joy that passes all understanding.

Many people have been inspired by the joyful spirit of Mother Teresa. For example, a nurse who sees a lot of human suffering tries hard to present a cheerful, upbeat spirit to her patients. A father with a rather pessimistic outlook on life tries not to project that attitude on his children, while showing by example how his faith sustains him. A widow, who still grieves deeply the loss of her beloved husband, attempts to maintain a joyful spirit around her grandchildren.

What can I learn from Mother Teresa about the practice of Christian joy?

28. EMBRACING LIFE'S CROSSES

In the opening chapter of 1 Corinthians (vv. 22–25), Paul presents the essence of his preaching: "We proclaim Christ crucified." After his previous attempt to use a clever argument with the Athenians about their unknown god had produced only ridicule, the Apostle resolved to preach Jesus Christ and him crucified. This approach, however, had its own challenges. His Jewish audience, with a long tradition of connecting God's presence with marvelous signs, as in the exodus event, was looking for evidence to support Paul's preaching on the crucified Christ. His Gentile audience, on the other hand, expected rational philosophical arguments to support claims and ethical demands. As Paul put it, his message was "a stumbling block to Jews and foolishness to Gentiles." He went on to insist that, for believers, the rejected and despised Christ is truly in "the power of God and the wisdom of God." This means that "the foolishness of God is wiser than human wisdom, and the weakness of

God is stronger than human strength." God's ways are not our ways.

The fundamental Christian message has a paradoxical character. The death of Jesus on the cross, which appears to spell defeat for his mission, is a victory over the dark forces, including death itself. Crucifixion, which the Romans used to control conquered people, became the instrument of salvation and liberation for all human beings. The cross, so widely displayed and deeply revered by Christian people, symbolizes the essential truth of the gospel, which challenges worldly wisdom and naïve religious assumptions. God is not a harsh judge to be feared but a compassionate Father who lavishes unconditional love on all people. The God who did not intervene to save Jesus from the cross does not intervene in human affairs but offers us the strength to bear life's crosses. Jesus, who exemplified self-sacrificing love throughout his whole life, was not a utopian dreamer but a wise teacher who guides us on the path to full human development and fruitful engagement with the world. To embrace the cross is to reject the use of coercive power while committing ourselves to a life of self-sacrificing love that attends to our neighbors in need. No one completely embraces the cross. All of us can do a better job of appropriating Paul's message.

A wife who uses subtle coercion to dominate her husband could start treating him with greater love and respect. A father who still exercises too much influence over his married daughter could let go and give her space to live her own life. A mother who is angry at God because her prayers for her wayward son have gone unanswered could come to trust that God loves her son even more than she does. A community organizer who sometimes allows his desire for acclaim to get in the way of his work could purify his motives and serve the marginalized with greater self-giving love.

In what concrete way can I embrace the cross more fully?

29. RELYING ON GOD'S ENCOURAGEMENT

We can all use an encouraging word from time to time, especially when our faith is tried. In 2 Thessalonians 2:16—3:5, Paul prays that God will encourage and strengthen the Christian community in Thessalonica to persevere in doing good. "May our Lord Jesus Christ himself and God our Father, who has loved us and given us everlasting encouragement and good hope through his grace, encourage your hearts and strengthen them in every good deed and word." These verses identify Jesus as the "Christ," the anointed one, the promised Messiah, and as "Lord," the title given to Yahweh in the Hebrew Scriptures, suggesting he shares in the power of God. By his death and resurrection, Christ has made available to us an unlimited reservoir of encouragement and strength. Through prayer, we open our minds and hearts to receive what we need from this renewable energy source.

The second part of this passage has Paul asking for prayers that "the word of the Lord may speed forward" and "we may be delivered from perverse and wicked people." He is thinking of his mission to the Gentiles and praying that the gospel, which has an intrinsic dynamic power of its own, will draw increasing numbers of faithful believers into fellowship with Christ. The "wicked people," perhaps enemies who have tried to thwart his mission, remind us that we can expect opposition when trying to live the gospel in our contemporary world.

Such opposition is one reason we all need encouragement in our effort to be faithful Christians. We can get weary constantly battling our personal demons. Lovers and friends can disappoint us. Monstrous evil can overwhelm us. Political polarization and gridlock can tempt us to cynicism. Financial problems can lead to sleepless nights. Church scandals can generate rage and resentment. Unanswered prayers can lead to doubts. Slow spiritual progress can breed impatience.

As we face our personal depressants, we can try to appropriate the good news in this passage, drawing on God's "everlasting encouragement" and the "good hope" Christ has won for us. For many years Prisca confessed gossiping as her major sin in her annual Lenten celebration of the sacrament of penance, no longer even hoping to overcome it. One year the priest suggested a penance that each day during the coming month she do two things: ask Christ to help her speak positively of others and pay someone an honest compliment. She accepted the penance, did it faithfully for a month, and was so pleased with the progress on her long-standing fault that she made the penance a regular part of her daily effort to live the law of love.

Saul was so upset by the clergy sex abuse scandal that he left his parish and stopped going to Mass. He read an article by a theologian pointing out that Catholics who leave the Church lose the power to reform it. After praying for Christ's guidance, Saul decided to reconnect with his parish and became very active in a movement to get greater lay involvement in dealing with the scandal.

Samson was so frustrated by the gridlock in Washington that he did not vote in the midterm election. After hearing a homily on the responsibility of good citizenship, he decided not only to vote in the next election but also to actively support candidates who best represent Catholic social teaching.

Have I experienced God's "everlasting encouragement" in my own life?

30. IMPROVING CHRISTIAN-JEWISH RELATIONSHIPS

With the current alarming rise of anti-Semitism, it is especially important for Christians to take the initiative in denouncing prejudice and improving relations with the Jewish community. Romans 11:13–32 includes a classic statement on this relationship. Paul is trying to make sense of the distressing fact that almost three decades after the death of Jesus, the Jewish people have still not accepted him as the promised Messiah. Writing to Gentile Christians in Rome, Paul declared that he glories in his role as Apostle to the Gentiles "in order to make my race jealous and thus save some of them." Paul goes on to make the argument that just as the Jewish rejection led to the outreach to the Gentiles, so the Gentiles' conversion to Christ will lead to Jewish acceptance of Christ. Paul's articulation of his argument can be difficult to follow so I have added to the text some explanatory names and phrases: "Just as you [Gentiles] once disobeyed God but have now received mercy [accepted Christ] because of their [Jews] disobedience, so they [Jews] have now disobeyed [rejected Christ] in order that, by virtue of the mercy shown to you [conversion of Gentiles], they too [Jews] may [now] receive mercy [the grace to accept Christ]."

In the middle of his argument, Paul makes this remarkable statement about the initial election of the Jews: God's gifts and his call are "irrevocable." In other words, the Jews remain God's chosen people, heirs of the promise, with a continuing role to play in the divine plan of salvation. Paul concludes this passage with a hopeful statement of universal salvation: "For

God delivered all to disobedience, that he might have mercy upon all."

In its Declaration on Non-Christian Religions, Vatican II makes explicit reference to today's epistle (no. 4). The declaration acknowledges that Christianity has its roots in the Jewish tradition, that Christ descended from the Israelites, and that the first apostles were of Jewish descent. It affirms Paul's teaching that "the Jews remain very dear to God" and looks forward to that day when Christians and Jews together will call on God with one voice. In a carefully worded statement, the declaration insists "neither all Jews indiscriminately of that time, nor Jews today, can be charged with the crimes committed during his [Jesus's] passion." The Church is the new people of God, but "the Jews should not be spoken of as rejected or accursed as if this followed from Holy Scriptures." The Church "deplores all hatreds, persecutions, displays of anti-Semitism leveled at any time or from any source against the Jews." Positively, the Council encourages mutual understanding between Christians and Jews through "biblical and theological inquiry and through friendly discussions."

Our charge today is to further efforts to improve relationships between the Jewish and Catholic communities. Here are some possibilities: Catholic religious education programs could be extra careful to avoid all anti-Semitic language. Interfaith dialogue programs could make sure Jewish representatives are invited to participate. Pastors could preach more homilies that include the assigned passages from the Hebrew Scriptures. Catholic parishes interested in sponsoring Passover meals could first find out if they violate Jewish sensibilities. Christian families could befriend Jewish families in the neighborhood. Christian religious studies majors could take a course on Judaism. Christians could support Jewish efforts to honor Righteous Gentiles. Christians interested in promoting peace between

Palestinians and Israelites could be more attentive to the diverse views within both sides.

What can I do to promote better relationships between Christians and Jews?

31. SEIZING OPPORTUNITIES FOR SPIRITUAL GROWTH

Our daily lives, mundane as they might be, are filled with opportunities to grow in holiness by loving God and neighbor. The Letter to the Ephesians (5:15–20) offers this advice: "Watch carefully then how you live, not as foolish persons but as wise, making the most of the opportunity, because the days are evil." To take full advantage of opportunities, we must "try to understand what is the will of the Lord." In discerning the divine will, we should stay sober and with a clear head draw on the wisdom and energy of the Holy Spirit. Common public prayer with hymns and spiritual songs, along with private prayer in our hearts, puts us in touch with the Holy Spirit, who guides our efforts to seize the moment and make the most of our opportunities. For these moments of grace and for all blessings, we should give "thanks always and for everything in the name of our Lord Jesus Christ to God the Father."

Our daily lives are filled with opportunities to do God's will by growing spiritually, attending to our neighbors in need and serving the common good. There are various reasons for failing to take advantage of these opportunities: we are too busy, too distracted, too self-centered, and too superficial. We may lack some specific knowledge that would alert us to the rich potential of daily opportunities: for instance, we may not realize that ordinary experience has a depth dimension or that life provides a path to holiness. Good Christians may have such an underdeveloped appreciation of the role of the Holy Spirit that they cannot imagine the Spirit at work in their daily activities. It is possible for us to take the simple blessings of life so much for granted that we fail to see them as catalysts for prayers and spiritual growth.

Let us imagine individuals who surmount these obstacles and move forward, making the most of the opportunities encountered on the journey of life. Tim, a busy, hard-driving lawyer with multiple demands on his time, could rethink his priorities and find more opportunities to be present for his family. Tina, who often feels underappreciated for her demanding job of raising three kids, could find deeper meaning in her motherly responsibilities by seeing them as her path to holiness. Mark, a faithful Catholic with a strong devotion to Christ present in the Eucharist, could enrich his spiritual life by listening to the Holy Spirit calling him to do more to help persons in need. Mary, who has generally taken for granted her excellent education, successful career, and happy marriage, could come to see them as undeserved blessings, a graced insight leading to prayers of gratitude and greater appreciation of the simple gifts of everyday life.

How can I take better advantage of the specific opportunities for growth and service that come my way?

32. RESPECTING GOD'S WAYS

Among believers there is always the danger of distorting our relationship to God: thinking we can define and control God to explain or defend the divine plan, confining our prayers to petitions while neglecting praise and thanksgiving, and forgetting that God remains ultimately mysterious beyond our thoughts and images. Romans 11:33–36 provides an inspiring safeguard against making God in our image.

In that passage, Paul offers a marvelous rapturous hymn of praise to God who remains the ultimately mysterious source, agent, and goal of salvation for all. "Oh, the depth of the riches and wisdom and knowledge of God! How inscrutable are his judgments and how unsearchable his ways!" As limited human beings, we cannot fully comprehend God's plan of salvation or adequately explain the role of the Jewish people in it. We can praise and thank the gracious God for extending mercy and forgiveness to all people.

Quoting scripture, Paul reinforces his point with two rhetorical questions: "For who has known the mind of the Lord or who has been his counselor? Or who has given him anything that he may be repaid?" It is not up to us to demand an explanation from God. Our task is to accept God's will as it unfolds in our experience and to cooperate with divine grace in extending the kingdom of salvation in our world.

We can imagine some positive responses to this passage from Romans. An elderly woman: "I want that uplifting prayer read at my funeral." A young adult: "I am going to include more praise of God in my daily prayers." An engineer: "I am reminded that some things in life are beyond human reasoning." A secretary: "Reflecting on that passage lifts my heart in prayer." An architect: "I have to get over my anger at God for not answering my prayers." A religious sister: "I can see that I have fallen into the modern trap of expecting God to justify her plans to my satisfaction."

How does Paul's hymn of praise touch my mind and heart?

33. MAINTAINING OUR SPIRITUAL BALANCE

In struggling to maintain a stable disposition amid the ups and downs of life, we can find inspiration in the life and words of Paul the Apostle as found in Philippians 4:12–20. Around the year AD 50, Paul, traveling with his fellow missionaries Silas and Timothy, crossed the sea from present-day Turkey to Greece, going on to the historic Roman city of Philippi, where in 42 BC, Mark Antony and Octavian had defeated Brutus and Cassius, the assassins of Julius Caesar, and later settled the veterans of their victorious armies. Despite imprisonment and torture, Paul courageously preached the gospel of Christ to the Philippians, converting many, including a businesswoman by the name of Lydia who allowed him to stay in her house. Paul maintained very warm relationships with the Philippian community, the first Christian church established in Europe.

Years later, while in prison (perhaps in Ephesus around AD 56) Paul wrote a letter to his beloved Philippians. In a passage, taken from the end of that letter, Paul thanks his friends for their kindness in his "distress," perhaps some assistance during his imprisonment. He places his expression of gratitude in the larger context of his absolute trust in God, who called him to preach the gospel and supported his efforts in all circumstances good and bad. His trusting faith enabled him to maintain an inner equilibrium when his ministry brought him humiliation as well as adulation. As Paul put it, he learned the "secret of being well fed and of going hungry." That secret, which he shared with his Philippian friends and with us, is that God will supply whatever we need to carry out our God-given tasks and responsibilities. Life can feel like a roller coaster between highs and lows, between surpassing joys and profound sorrows, between simple pleasures and major disappointments. In the midst of such ups and downs, Paul wants us to maintain a spiritual balance, a calm acceptance of reality, and an emotional strength rooted in a fundamental trust in the God who loves, supports, forgives, and guides us in all circumstances.

We can imagine individuals drawing inspiration and guidance from the Apostle Paul. A secretary working for a mercurial boss could refuse to allow his dark moods to affect her own natural sunny disposition. A husband shaken by a wife's sudden decision to abandon him and their children could learn over time to forgive her while dedicating himself to helping the children manage the stress of the divorce. A woman who successfully managed the trauma of surgery, chemo, and radiation for breast cancer and gratefully enjoyed two years of good health could once again, with God's grace, courageously accept and fight a second diagnosis of cancer. A man deeply distressed by the polarized politics in our country could rise above his disappointment and become active in local politics. A sports fan who gets overly distraught when his favorite teams lose could get a more balanced perspective on sports and find greater satisfaction in being a good husband and father.

What concrete step could I take to maintain a more balanced inner life?

34. TRUSTING GOD'S WILL TO SAVE ALL PEOPLE

As we ponder the fate of those who have completed their earthly journey, we read in 1 Timothy 2:4–8 that God "wills everyone to be saved" and that Christ Jesus "gave himself as ransom for all." Can we indeed trust God's will to save all people? In the history of the Church, there was a long tradition of "no salvation outside the Church," taught by theologians and solemnly declared by popes. Nevertheless, in one of the most striking and consequential examples of the development of Christian doctrine in the whole history of the Church, the Second Vatican Council (1962–65) officially taught a remarkable version of salvation optimism. The Dogmatic Constitution on the Church, one of the most important of the sixteen conciliar documents, referencing 1 Timothy declared, "Those also can attain to everlasting salvation who through no fault of their own do not know the gospel of Christ or His Church, yet sincerely seek God and, moved by grace, strive by their deeds to do His will as it is known to them through the dictates of conscience. Nor does divine Providence deny the help necessary for salvation to those who, without blame on their part, have not yet arrived at an explicit knowledge of God, but who strive to live a good life, thanks to His grace" (Abbott translation, no. 16). In other words, even atheists can be saved if they follow their conscience. This means the Catholic Church, often accused of a narrowly restricted outlook on salvation, now officially has a most open and inclusive teaching on God's will to save all people.

This indeed is good news for many Catholics: those who intuitively think no salvation outside the Church is too restrictive; those who believe that their good Jewish and Muslim friends will be saved; those who wonder about the salvation of their deceased atheistic and agnostic relatives; those who worry about the ultimate fate of their good-hearted but nonpracticing children and grandchildren; and those who suffer from scrupulosity and fear eternal damnation.

How does Catholic salvation optimism impact my spiritual life?

35. ATTEMPTING TO BE WORTHY OF THE GOSPEL

As Christians we are blessed to have the gospel as a guide, the good news of Jesus Christ to direct and gladden our lives. Our ongoing challenge is to treasure this good news and strive for the high ideals of the gospel. The Apostle

Paul deals with this challenge in Philippians 1:20–24. Writing from prison (probably in Ephesus around AD 56), Paul expresses his gratitude to the Philippians for their continuing support. He goes on to muse about whether he prefers to die now and be with Jesus Christ or to continue his earthly ministry of proclaiming the gospel. Caught between these two options, he writes, "I long to depart this life and be with Christ, [for] that is far better. Yet that I remain [in] the flesh is more necessary for your benefit." For Paul, "life is Christ," which means that serving the Lord is his passion, the motivation that guides his decisions, the driving force that propels his ministry. He notes that "Christ will be magnified in my body." In other words, the Lord will be honored and glorified in and through his everyday life of service in the real world of personal encounters. In verse 27, Paul offers some important guidance: "Only, conduct yourselves in a way worthy of the gospel of Christ."

Perhaps the Apostle's counsel takes on greater significance for us when we consider his own human struggle to discern God's will for him. Despite his desire to be with Christ forever, he did act in a way worthy of the gospel by devoting himself totally to preaching the good news to the ends of the world, until his plans to visit Spain were thwarted by his martyrdom in Rome, sometime between 64 and 67.

Inspired by Paul's example, we too should strive to live in a way worthy of the gospel. Of course, no human effort is ever a completely worthy response to the free gift of salvation God grants to us through the death and resurrection of Christ. But that only encourages us to do our best. A teacher tries to extend his natural affection for some of his students to a deeper concern for all of them. A family physician returns to the poor neighborhood where she grew up to set up her practice. A coach takes on the added responsibility of helping his players make it as good persons and productive citizens.

A woman who was baptized Catholic during her collegiate years finds appropriate ways of sharing her faith with her nonpracticing, nominally Catholic parents.

What could I do to conduct myself in a way worthy of the gospel?

36. ENDURING OUR TRIALS AS DISCIPLINE

It can be misleading to simply repeat biblical admonitions developed in a very different cultural context. For example, in Hebrews 12:5–13, the unknown author quotes Proverbs 3:11–12: "My son, do not disdain the discipline of the Lord or lose heart when reproved by him; for whom the Lord loves, he disciplines," and then adds an admonition, "Endure your trials as 'discipline.'" To explain his point, the author compares God's discipline to a good father who disciplines his son, which is painful but produces "the peaceful fruit of righteousness." The God who disciplines us as sons and daughters thereby strengthens our "drooping hands" and "weak knees" and makes "straight paths" for our feet.

Today, we are more aware of the dangers of misinterpreting this passage. God does not inflict suffering on us to teach us a lesson about life. Human suffering is not a punishment from God for sinful actions. Those who imagine God as a harsh judge or severe disciplinarian tend to have low self-esteem that impedes healthy spiritual development.

Suffering is an unavoidable part of human existence. We all know something of the suffering involved in emotional distress, physical illness, moral failures, and the dark boundary of death. Some suffering is so horrendous and monstrous that anything said beyond silent compassion and healing embrace feels glib and disrespectful. On the other hand, we know good Christians who testify to the teaching of Hebrews that we should endure our trials as discipline, as instructive training for life. They have found a way to view their suffering not as a divine punishment or test but as an opportunity to come closer to God.

Some examples come to mind. Ed, a hard-driving corporate executive who was overweight and spiritually undernourished, suffered a heart attack. After surgery and recovery, he expressed gratitude to God by making important changes in his life: returning to his earlier practice of regular Sunday Mass, maintaining a better balance between work and family life, exercising regularly and eating properly, and saying brief prayers throughout his still busy days.

Ida worked for over ten years as a secretary for a large advertising firm. She liked her job, made an above-average salary, enjoyed the respect of her colleagues, and got along with her immediate boss. Then the firm hired a new manager who took a special interest in her. At first she felt flattered, but then he became more aggressive, making flirtatious comments, telling her crude jokes, touching her inappropriately, and even suggesting they have a mutually beneficial affair. At each point, she clearly and firmly told him she was not interested, but inside she was churning with intense feelings of guilt, shame, fear, and doubt about what to do. Her distressing situation prompted her to take action: telling her husband and a few friends, learning more about the prevalence of sex abuse in the workplace, reading about the Me Too movement, reflecting on stories of victims, and asking God for guidance. When Ida finally took the courageous step of telling her boss, she felt a sense of inner peace that she did the right thing no matter what happened next.

Can I recall a time when suffering led to personal growth?

37. MANAGING OUR ANXIETY

In trying to deal with the inevitable stresses, worry, and anxiety built into human life, we can find good advice in Philippians 4:6–9. Writing from prison to his beloved Christian community in Philippi, the Apostle Paul offers them advice on how to deal with anxiety, perhaps caused by persecution or an external threat. "Have no anxiety at all, but in everything, by prayer and petition, with thanksgiving, make your requests known to God." Whatever the cause of their anxiety, the answer is prayer that asks for God's help and expresses gratitude for all gifts received. Prayer does not automatically eliminate threats, but it does remind us that God remains with us in stressful circumstances—a comforting thought that can reduce anxiety. Prayer can build up our confidence that divine grace is more powerful than all the evil forces that assault us. Developing a balanced prayer life that includes both petitions and expressions of gratitude prepares us for the gift of God's peace, as Paul indicates: "Then the peace of God that surpasses all understanding will guard your hearts and minds in Christ Jesus." This peace, which protects us against undue anxiety, is not simply the absence of conflict, but a deep, abiding sense of inner harmony that results from being in tune with God's will.

To prepare for God's gift of peace, Paul advises us to reflect on high ideals: whatever is true, honorable, lovely, gracious, excellent, and worthy of praise. In addition to thinking lofty thoughts, the Apostle advises, "Keep on doing what you have learned and received and heard and seen in me. Then the God of peace will be with you." Paul claims we will find peace by following the example of Christ who trusted God totally, by reflecting on virtues that lift our spirits, and by adopting a prayer routine that includes requests for God's help and thanksgiving for favors received.

We can think of individuals who have cooperated with God's grace and know something of the peace that passes understanding. As a young woman before she got married, Lydia had an abortion that she hid from her parents and her husband. A couple of years into her marriage she began to suffer from anxiety. She talked about it with her pastor who suggested she celebrate the sacrament of reconciliation and tell her husband about the abortion. After a very honest confession and a tearful conversation with her understanding spouse, she felt a deep inner peace that she had never known before in her life, a blessing that led to prayers of gratitude.

Jonah, an ambitious executive, dealt with the great stress of work by consuming copious amounts of vodka after he got home to his bachelor condo. Surprisingly touched by an Ash Wednesday homily on doing a constructive Lenten penance, he prayed for guidance and committed himself to a strict Lenten regime: exercising each day after work at a local health club, limiting alcohol consumption to one drink a day, and visiting twice a week his elderly aunt who was confined to a nursing home. By Easter, Jonah was convinced that his Lenten regimen was a better way of handling work stress than numbing his anxiety with alcohol.

In what specific ways can my Christian faith help me better manage the anxiety that threatens my inner peace?

Chapter Four

Christian Conversion

We can find a christocentric element, implied or explicit, in the first three conversions. For example, intellectual conversion can look to Christ as the wisdom of the Father and the wisest of teachers. Moral conversion finds its supreme law in Christ's command to love our neighbor as ourselves. Religious conversion calls us to respond to God's love most completely manifested in sending his son Jesus Christ, our Lord, into the world to save all of us.

The meditations in this chapter are more explicitly christocentric. For us, Christ is himself the parable of God's love and the clearest manifestation of divine love. He is also the exemplar of fulfilled humanity and the best the human race has produced. He is the absolute savior and the definitive prophet, the supreme icon of divine glory, the great protagonist of the marvelous drama of salvation authored by God, and the fullness of divine truth. Christian conversion involves a process of deepening our commitment to Christ, appropriating his teaching, and following his example in our everyday lives.

1. MAKING CHRIST OUR KING

In our fast-paced world with its competing demands, it can be difficult to maintain the reign of Christ over our minds and hearts. First Corinthians 15:20–28 encourages us to stay focused on Christ and his resurrection as the core of the gospel, the fundamental conviction of Christian faith, and the basis for our hope in the final triumph of good over evil. Paul begins this passage with a brief statement of this belief: "Christ has been raised from the dead, the firstfruits of those who have fallen asleep." He then suggests an analogy: "For just as in Adam all die, so too in Christ shall all be brought to life." Finally, the Apostle describes an ordered process: Christ "the firstfruits" delivers the kingdom to his Father after subjecting all his enemies, including death, "the last enemy," so that "God may be all in all."

Throughout the passage, Paul uses language that suggests the kingship of Christ. He is the one who saves "those who belong to [him]," who "must reign," "who hands over the kingdom to his God and Father," and who has everything "subjected to him." The risen Christ is the universal King, the cosmic Lord, the Savior of all.

Christians find diverse ways of making Christ the King of their lives. His kingdom is multidimensional, taking many legitimate forms. There are various degrees of commitment to the crucified and risen Lord. Some believers can express their belief in Christ the King with great ease and precision, while others are more reticent and less articulate. The Christian community is enriched by all those who are willing to share something of the way Christ reigns in their lives. A truck driver, who uses his long hours on the road for periods of prayerful reflection, speaks openly with his wife and best friend about his daily efforts to let Christ rule his life. A lawyer faced with complex ethical questions has trained herself to reflect on what Jesus would do in those situations. A Marine made it through his rigorous training by imagining Jesus on the cross, speaking words of encouragement to him. A grandmother who often attends Mass during the week thinks of her Amen when receiving communion as saying yes to sharing in the mission of Christ to extend God's reign in the world.

In what concrete ways does Christ function as King of my life?

2. RECOGNIZING CHRIST IN THE EUCHARIST AND THE NEEDY

In our ongoing efforts to maintain the essential unity of love of God and love of neighbor, we can find a crucial theological insight in 1 Corinthians 11:23–26, which provides us with the earliest account of the institution of the Eucharist at the Last Supper. Handing on a liturgical tradition he received, Paul recalls that Jesus, on the night he was betrayed, took bread, gave thanks, broke it, and said, "This is my body that is for you. Do this in remembrance of me." The Apostle goes on to recall Jesus saying, "This cup is the new covenant in my blood. Do this, as often as you drink it, in remembrance of me." Paul concludes this passage: "For as often as you eat this bread and drink the cup, you proclaim the death of the Lord until he comes."

Paul intended this passage as a response to a troubling practice in the Corinthian community. It seems that the Christian converts gathered for Eucharist in the homes of wealthy members, where the affluent ate and drank excessively while the poor went hungry. Paul is pointing out that this practice violates the meaning of the Eucharist, which celebrates the generous self-giving love of Christ.

For Paul, the Eucharist is a memorial meal that recalls and re-presents, or makes present again, the death and resurrection of Christ. At the Last Supper, Christ performed a prophetic gesture, offering himself through the ritual of sharing bread and wine in an anticipation of his total self-giving on the cross that led to his glorious resurrection.

When we gather for the Eucharist today, we not only remember Christ's life of self-sacrificing love but also commit ourselves to sharing in his mission to spread the kingdom of love and justice in the world. Recognizing Christ's presence in the consecrated bread and wine should lead us to see him in the hungry and thirsty and those who suffer from discrimination and injustice. Our remembrance of Christ at Mass unites love of God and love of neighbor, reflective worship, and charitable deeds.

Ideally, parishes put this understanding of the Eucharist into practice. For example: the social justice committee puts a peace or justice action alert in the parish bulletin each week; the pastor makes use of Catholic social teaching in his homilies; parishioners run a food distribution center to feed the hungry in the area; the congregation participates in the annual clothing drive to help the needy; the liturgy committee includes a prayer for charitable causes in the prayer of the faithful; the parish energetically promotes the Catholic Campaign for Human Development; the Bread for the World committee lobbies Congress for legislation to help feed the hungry; families strive to overcome discrimination in their own limited sphere of influence; individuals find creative ways to promote justice and peace in the world.

How can I contribute to the social ministry of my parish?

3. PROMOTING PARISH UNITY

Unfortunately, a healthy Catholic pluralism sometimes devolves into destructive polarization. For us Catholics, it is important that our celebration of the eucharistic liturgy be perceived not as a battleground but as a common ground that brings us closer together. In this regard, let us reflect on 1 Corinthians 10:16–17, where Paul proposes two rhetorical questions: "The cup of blessing that we bless, is it not a participation in the blood of Christ? The bread that we break, is it not a participation in the body of Christ?" Jesus instituted the Eucharist at the Last Supper in the context of a Jewish Passover meal that included a "cup of blessing," the cup of wine shared at the end of the meal accompanied by a blessing over the meal. By sharing in the cup, Christians participate in the blood of Christ poured out in his death on the cross. By participating in the eucharistic breaking of the bread, we are incorporated into the Body of Christ. At Mass we become what we eat, the Body of Christ, the Church.

Paul concludes the passage: "Because the loaf of bread is one, we, though many, are one body, for we all partake of the one loaf." Throughout his correspondence with the Corinthians, Paul emphasizes the need for unity because they are suffering from divisive rivalries. The Eucharist by its very nature unites us with Christ and with one another. In Christ, we are all brothers and sisters. The liturgy celebrates this unity and promotes it. Participating in Mass regularly should bring us closer to Christ and to our fellow parishioners. We may differ on secondary matters of piety and theology, but we are united in our common commitment to Christ. *Corpus Christi* has two meanings: The eucharistic bread and the Church as the Body of Christ. We could think of our "Amen" when we receive communion as an affirmation of the real presence of Christ and of our obligation to work for the unity of the Church.

We know examples of parishioners contributing to parish unity. In an affluent suburban parish, the chair of the social justice committee and the leader of a pro-life group cosponsored a shared evening of reflection that included prayer and informal discussions. An inner-city parish with a mix of white, black, and Hispanic parishioners sponsored a series of discussions during Lent on the challenges faced by each group. In a university parish, permanent community members interact with collegians in various ways: preparing them for marriage, hosting them for home meals, and mentoring of individual students by faculty members in their field. In a rural parish, two women succeeded in getting their pastor to be more inclusive of women and their concerns in his homilies.

What can I do to promote unity in my parish?

4. DRAWING ON THE LIBERATING POWER OF THE RESURRECTION

As Christians striving for an integrated understanding of our faith, we focus on the paschal mystery, the death and resurrection of Christ. The resurrection gives meaning to the cross. Easter reveals the significance of Good Friday. Our belief in the risen Christ enriches our spiritual life in many ways. On the great liturgical Feast of Easter, 1 Corinthians 5:6–8 interprets the resurrection of Christ from the perspective of the exodus event commemorated at the Jewish Passover meal. By the time of Jesus, the Jews celebrated their liberation from bondage in Egypt with a sacred meal that included unleavened bread and roasted lamb. As part of the

CONVERSION AS A WAY OF LIFE

Passover celebration, pious Jews disposed of the old bread leavened by yeast, which they considered corrupt, and baked new unleavened bread, symbolizing a new purified life. The roasted lamb reminded them of the exodus when God commanded the Israelite families in Egypt to slaughter a lamb, sprinkle the blood on their doorposts, roast the lamb, and eat it in haste, ready to depart Egypt (Exod 12:1–30).

Drawing on this symbolism, Paul instructs us, "Clear out the old yeast, so that you may become a fresh batch of dough." Since Christ, our paschal lamb, has been sacrificed, we should celebrate, not with the old yeast of "malice and wickedness," but with the "unleavened bread of sincerity and truth."

By linking Easter and the exodus, the epistle invites reflection on the liberating power of the death and resurrection of Christ. In Luke's Gospel, Jesus began his public ministry by presenting himself as a liberator who will free the captives and preach the good news to the poor. In his personal interactions, he freed individuals from their fears, guilt, and isolation. He healed lepers confined to the outskirts, freeing them to return to their families and friends. He liberated women from their social isolation and included them in his preaching and mission. His preaching called for forgiveness and reconciliation that breaks the cycle of violence and recrimination. Through his death and resurrection, Christ extended his liberating power to all people, in all times and all places.

By liberating us from all that enslaves us, Christ freed us for personal growth, for serving others, for contributing to society, for promoting the common good, and for extending the reign of God in this world. The resurrection proclaims the ultimate defeat of all the forces that impede, limit, and confine the human spirit and celebrates the final triumph of Christ's liberating grace, which brings us full human development. Christ, the paschal lamb, has given us a fresh start so we can put aside the enslaving patterns of the past and enjoy the new life of authentic freedom.

We can imagine people who can benefit from this liberating message: the married woman who still feels guilty over a teenage abortion, the collegian struggling to escape the drug culture, the executive caught up in the whirlwind of frenetic activity, the social worker overwhelmed by an excessive caseload, the citizen fighting cynicism over partisan polarization, the parishioner who feels unfairly constrained by the pastor and his staff, and the pastor who feels burdened by administrative responsibilities. Human existence is inevitably limited, which means the resurrection, with its liberating power, is good news for everyone, including ourselves.

In what specific way can the resurrection of Christ be liberating for me?

5. MAINTAINING A RESURRECTION PERSPECTIVE

The Christian community is still in the process of appropriating the teachings of Vatican II, including the notion of the "hierarchy of truths," which means some doctrines are more important than others. The Council taught that the resurrection is the most significant Christian doctrine, the core belief that God raised the crucified Jesus to the glorified life of the risen Christ. Belief in the resurrection provides a perspective for understanding and living the whole Christian life. For example, Colossians 3:1–4 tells us, "If then you were raised with Christ, seek what is above," and adds, "Think of what is above, not of what is on earth." Through our baptism we died with Christ and rose with him to share in his glorified life. The risen Christ is now seated at the right hand of God, where he intercedes on our behalf. When Christ appears to complete his saving mission, we will share in his glory.

This passage makes a sharp distinction between what is above, where the glorified Lord dwells, and what is on earth, where we dwell. The text does say that we are to think about and seek heavenly things and not earthly matters, but it does not mean that we are to spend all day praying while neglecting our daily needs and responsibilities. It does, however, serve as a reminder to maintain a proper Christian perspective on our life in this world. Faith in the risen Lord encourages us to value and respect earthly matters, without turning them into absolutes or idols that distort their meaning and inflate their value. It celebrates the deeper meaning of everyday life in this world and energizes us for the task of doing our part to humanize our life on planet Earth.

We can all find ways to appropriate the developments encouraged by a resurrection perspective: greater respect for the body that shares in the final victory; a clearer sense that the path to holiness passes through everyday life; a deeper understanding that our work has intrinsic value because it contributes to the building of the eternal kingdom; greater confidence that our deceased loved ones now live with God; a deeper appreciation that our earthly joys are a foretaste of heavenly delight; a more profound conviction that our earthly journey brings us to final union with the risen Christ.

In what specific way does a resurrection perspective promote my spiritual growth?

6. FOCUSING ON THE RESURRECTION

In trying to maintain a proper focus in our spiritual life it is helpful to remember that the best of the Christian tradition has always centered on following Jesus Christ and participating in his death and resurrection. It has made the resurrection the central Christian doctrine and Easter the primary liturgical celebration. Maintaining and explaining this focus has been challenging. The tradition has two main ways to speak about God raising the crucified Jesus to life: one, the many appearances of the risen Christ to the disciples, including Mary of Magdala, Peter known as Cephas, Thomas the Twin, and Cleopas with his companion; and the other, the empty tomb stories as reported by Mary Magdalene.

There are other ways of interpreting the resurrection. For example, Colossians 3:1–4 speaks of Christ "seated at the right hand of God." The Father has raised the man Jesus to life and taken him to heaven, where he sits at God's right hand. The Word who descended from heaven has now ascended back to God. With the ascension of the Lord, our human nature now has a permanent place in the heavenly realm.

Seated at God's right hand, Christ permanently exercises his priesthood, interceding on our behalf, presiding over the extension of God's reign in the world, and serving as the high priest in the liturgy of the Church. As the risen Lord, he is the mediator between God and us, our access to the Father. From his permanent position of power and influence, he will come to judge the living and the dead.

The passage from Colossians admonishes those of us raised with Christ to "think of what is above" and to "seek" heavenly things. We could hear this as a call to raise our hearts to God in prayer and to live the high ideals of the gospel. It is not a matter of ignoring the concerns of this world or disdaining everyday life. We are called to maintain a faith perspective on our personal journey and to follow Christian principles in dealing with social issues. We should live everyday life recognizing that we already participate in the risen life of Christ and will one day share in his final victory.

Our celebration of Easter can transform our lives. Jeff becomes more joyful when he reflects on sharing in the risen life of Christ. Mary becomes more confident when she remembers that the risen Christ intercedes for her as she faces the challenges of life. Bill becomes more loving when he reflects on the self-sacrificing love of Jesus that led to his death and glorious resurrection. Sue becomes more hopeful when she realizes that the Christ seated at the right hand of the Father defeated death, ensuring the final victory of good over evil.

How can celebrating the resurrection transform my life?

7. CARING FOR THE EARTH

In developing a Christian ecospirituality that accepts responsibility for protecting our planet, we can find a solid basis in Colossians 1:15–20, one of the New Testament's most significant and lyrical expressions of Christ's role in creation and its redemption. The passage, drawn from an early Christian hymn, portrays Christ Jesus as "the image of the invisible God, the firstborn of all creation." In him, through him, and for him "were created all things in heaven and on earth, the visible and the invisible." He is "before all things," the "firstborn from the dead," the "head of the body, the church," who holds all things together. Christ, who is "preeminent," reconciled all things, "making peace by the blood of his cross."

Throughout Christian history, this poetic passage has inspired reflection on the "cosmic Christ," who, like the personified figure of Wisdom in the Hebrew Scriptures, is the pattern for God's creative activity and the unifying center of the whole created world. He exercises sovereign authority over all creatures, including angelic beings (thrones, dominions, principalities), who, according to some false teachers among the Colossians, had control over human affairs and the created world.

From a modern scientific perspective, believers can see the cosmic Christ as the inner energy of the evolutionary process, propelling it toward its final fulfillment. He is the ultimate goal of the historical process, when the material world will share in Christ's victory over all the divisive forces by reconciling all things in himself.

This exalted view of Christ provides a solid foundation for a contemporary ecospirituality. As disciples of Christ, we have a moral responsibility to care for the earth, the common home for the whole human family. The material world, held together by the cosmic Lord, possesses a fundamental goodness that makes it worthy of our respect and care. Our calling is not to subdue and dominate the earth but to tend the earthly garden as good stewards. As the leading edge of the evolutionary process, we humans share in the mission of the cosmic Christ to lead the created world to its final fulfillment. Commitment to Christ, who is both the exemplar of full humanity and the Lord of the universe, moves us to protect our planet and all its life-forms.

A growing number of Christians recognize this responsibility and have acted on it. Parishes have sponsored studies of *Laudato Si'*, the encyclical by Pope Francis that deals with the environmental crisis. Families have become more careful about recycling. Couples have cut back on luxury consumption. Citizens have made environmental concerns part of their voting decisions. Students familiar with the dangers of climate change have shared their concerns with their parents. Individuals are doing their part by eating less red meat, using less electricity, and driving more fuel-efficient cars.

What specific steps could I take to help care for the environment?

8. DEVELOPING A BALANCED SPIRITUALITY

In the ongoing effort to develop and maintain an integrated and balanced Christian spirituality, short creeds that emphasize the fundamentals of the faith can be helpful. In 1 Corinthians 15:1–11, Paul offers such a brief summary of Christian faith: "For I handed on to you as of first importance what I also received: that Christ died for our sins in accordance with the scriptures; that he was buried; that he was raised on the third day in accordance with the scriptures; that he appeared to Cephas, then to the Twelve."

Let us examine the four components of this short creed, Christ died, was buried, was raised to life, and appeared to many. Jesus, the Word made flesh, shared fully in the human condition. From the moment of our conception, we are shadowed by death, the one inevitable event on our journey. Jesus did not seek death, but he did freely accept it as the by-product of absolute fidelity to the cause of God and humanity, which incurred the ire of the religious and political establishment. The death of Jesus is a commonly accepted historical fact. He was executed during the governorship of Pontius Pilate in or around AD 30 by crucifixion, the cruel form of capital punishment Rome commonly used to intimidate and control subjugated populations. For Paul, the death of Jesus fulfilled the promises of the Hebrew Scriptures and offered expiation for our sins. His short creed also affirms that Jesus was buried, indicating that he really did die and setting the stage for his resurrection on the third day.

Paul, who said nothing about the empty tomb tradition, concentrated on the fundamental affirmation that God raised Jesus on the third day, according to the scriptures. For Paul, Jesus did not raise himself to life, nor were there any eyewitnesses to the event. The risen Christ, however, did take the initiative and appeared to many disciples, including Paul himself. They became the witnesses to the reality and power of the death, burial, raising, and appearing of Christ.

In today's complex, busy, pluralistic, technological world, we need to concentrate on the fundamentals of our Christian faith. Given the knowledge explosion and the availability of diverse theological opinions, we need a firm grasp of the core gospel message. Paul's short creed reminds us that authentic Christian belief emphasizes both the death and the resurrection of Christ. Good Friday without Easter can lead to a heavy, somber piety that lacks joy. Resurrection without the cross can lead to a romantic, utopian spirituality that appears unrealistic. Reflecting on Paul's creed, Christians heavily burdened by life's crosses can find strength by embracing the risen Christ. Christians tempted to downplay the power of evil in the world can become more realistic by reflecting on the passion and death of Jesus.

What step could I take to develop a more balanced spirituality?

9. LIVING THE FAITH WE PROFESS

In our ongoing effort to live as authentic Christians who integrate word and deed, we can find encouragement in 1 John 3:18–24, which begins, "Children, let us love not in word or speech but in deed and truth." As members of God's family, we are called to love one another not just in what we say but especially in what we do and how we act. The traditional maxim that actions speak louder than words reflects this biblical truth. The community of the Beloved Disciple detected a fundamental deceit in saying we love God while treating our brothers and sisters hatefully (1 John 4:20). As Christians, we are called to live in the truth by practicing our faith, keeping our promises, and acting on our convictions.

CONVERSION AS A WAY OF LIFE

Love of God and love of neighbor are essentially connected and mutually reinforcing, as are prayer and charity. This truth grounds a moral imperative. Participating in Mass and receiving communion should move us to share in Christ's mission to extend the kingdom of God. Our private prayer life should attune us to the needs of our families, friends, and colleagues. Gratitude for God's blessings should move us to share them with others. The prayers of petition we offer for persons in need should alert us to concrete actions on their behalf. Feeling forgiven by God's mercy should move us to forgive those who have offended us. Learning more about Catholic social teaching should make us more active participants in spreading the reign of justice, peace, and love in this world. Participating regularly in a prayer group should nourish and inform our participation in the political process.

In striving to live authentic lives that integrate word and deed, Jesus Christ remains our model and guide. He was both the fullness of divine love and the epitome of human response. He lived and taught the fundamental unity of the love of God and love of neighbor. He reinforced his teachings on forgiveness by forgiving the executioners who nailed him to the cross. His personal authenticity made an impression on his followers and his opponents. His prayer life fueled his ministry. His memory continues to challenge his followers today who are tempted to divorce word and action.

Let us imagine a positive response to Christ's life and teaching. Sam, a cradle Catholic, never missed Sunday Mass, said a decade of the rosary each day, went to confession during Advent and Lent, led prayers before meals, participated in a monthly prayer group, and periodically gave informal moral instructions to his children. One Sunday, Sam heard a homily on loving God in deed and not just in word that triggered a conscious decision to try harder to practice what he professed. Instead of his usual habit of dominating the conversation while driving home from Mass, he began to elicit comments from his wife and children. He began to offer his decade of the rosary for a specific cause that he would then support financially. Instead of saying prayers for his penance when celebrating reconciliation, he agreed with the priest to do specific acts of charity. To strengthen his anti-drug message to his kids, he cut back on his alcohol consumption. He talked his prayer group into helping the parish Feed Your Neighbor program every other month. Grateful to God for his spiritual progress, Sam continues to look for more ways to integrate word and deed in his life.

How could I become a more integrated follower of Christ?

10. REFORMING OUR LIVES

Our culture today presents serious moral challenges to living a temperate Christian life, including the excesses of alcohol, drugs, hedonism, consumerism, and sexual license. To resist these temptations, we need a moral compass based on fundamental gospel values. In this regard, Paul's letter to the Romans encourages us to "throw off the works of darkness [and] put on the armor of light." The Apostle urges us to act properly, "not in orgies and drunkenness, not in promiscuity and licentiousness, not in rivalry and jealousy." Positively, he admonishes us to "put on the Lord Jesus Christ, and make no provision for the desires of the flesh," which is anything that detracts from following the guidance of the Spirit. It seems Paul expected the risen Christ to return soon to complete his saving work, making it imperative for his followers to move from the slumber of night to the mindfulness of day (Rom 13:11–14).

This passage from Romans played a key role in the conversion of St. Augustine (354–430). Sometime in 386, while teaching rhetoric in Milan, he had a deep conversation with his friend Alypius that led to an intense inner struggle over the direction of his life. Deeply agitated and weeping profusely, he went into a garden to be alone. There he heard a child's voice repeating "take and read," which he interpreted as a divine command to open the book of Paul's letters and read the first passage he saw: "not in orgies and drunkenness, not in promiscuity and licentiousness...but put on the Lord Jesus Christ." He no sooner finished the passage than relief from all guilt and shame flooded into his heart and "all the shadows of doubt were dispelled." Augustine went on to become a disciplined Christian, a dedicated bishop, an influential theologian, and a great saint.

The message from Romans can invite all of us to reform our lives and come closer to Christ. To the alcoholic, it says not in drunkenness but turn your life over to Christ and join AA. To the young man who spends too much time on internet porn sites, it says not in promiscuity but seek the Lord's help and develop healthier attitudes toward women and sex. To the woman who harbors a grudge against a former friend, it says not in rivalry but follow the example of Christ and initiate reconciliation. To the collegian who is envious of her roommate, it says not in jealousy but put on the mind of Christ and look for good qualities in her.

What moral conversion do I need in my own life?

11. EXPRESSING OUR FAITH IN CHRIST

Our Christian faith calls us not only to accept Christ in our hearts but also to express our faith publicly. Romans 10:9–13 invites reflection on this truth. "If you confess with your mouth that Jesus is Lord and believe in your heart that

God raised him from the dead, you will be saved." Paul elaborates on his major point: "No one who believes in him will be put to shame," adding that this is true for both Jews and Gentiles because there is one Lord of all.

We are justified and saved by faith in Christ as the "Lord," indicating his close union with the one God and his superiority over all earthly creatures. Our faith in Christ the Lord rests on the fundamental belief that God raised him from the dead. We are called not only to believe in the Lord in the privacy of our hearts but also to confess our belief publicly. Paul concludes the passage with a quote from the prophet Joel: "Everyone who calls on the name of the Lord will be saved."

The passage can help us develop a balanced approach to living the Christian life. The faith Paul urges is not an intellectual assent to certain revealed truths but a personal commitment to Christ as Lord and Savior, meaning we grow spiritually by following his example and teaching. We are saved not only by the death of Jesus on the cross but by his death and resurrection, which can help us live a more positive and joyful Christian life. The salvation Christ won for us is a free gift that cannot be earned or merited by our good works, a fundamental truth that can keep us humble and reduce our anxiety. Christianity is not a private philosophy of life but a total way of life that includes public expressions of faith. Authentic belief in the risen Christ leads to participation in his mission to spread the kingdom of justice and peace. The divine grace that justifies us seeks visibility. The Christian claim is more credible when belief leads to concrete acts of virtuous living.

We are blessed today with many ordinary witnesses to this faith: parents who instruct their children in the ways of the faith by what they say and especially how they act; workers who persevere at toilsome jobs to support their families;

citizens who rise above cynicism and continue to participate in the political process; parishioners who strive to make their parish a genuine community of faith, despite the sinfulness of the institutional Church.

How can I publicly live my faith in Christ the risen Lord?

12. HONORING THE CROSS OF CHRIST

For us Christians, the cross is a central symbol of our faith, representing Christ's definitive act of self-sacrificing love as well as his command to follow him by taking up the cross daily. At the end of his letter to the Galatians, Paul highlights the centrality of "the cross" in Christian faith and practice: "May I never boast except in the cross of our Lord Jesus Christ." Rehearsing a consistent theme in Galatians, he insists that the argument over whether male Gentile converts have to undergo the Jewish religious ritual of circumcision is not really a significant issue, because it is really through the death and resurrection of Christ that his disciples become a "new creation" characterized by "peace and mercy" for all. Striking a personal note, the Apostle says he bears the marks of the cross of Christ on his own body, a reference to the flogging he endured for proclaiming his faith in Christ crucified (Gal 6:14–18).

Christ's death on a cross was a heroic act of self-giving love, freely accepted as a by-product of his total commitment to the cause of God and humanity. As Christians, we are called to embrace the cross as the symbol of self-sacrificing love that judges all the idolatrous tendencies in our culture, for example, individualism, consumerism, sexism, xenophobia, racism, prejudice, militarism, and nationalism. Taking up the cross daily is a way of life, a fundamental feature of discipleship, a personal response to Christ's command.

In this, I still find inspiration in Fr. Bernard Boff, my seminary classmate, longtime friend, and fellow priest who went to his reward in 2013. I remember Bernie as a man who courageously embraced the crosses of daily life and as a priest with a cruciform heart, who had special compassion for victims of prejudice, exclusion, and injustice. In the early 1960s, he established the Bible Center in Toledo, which brought collegians from around the county to serve disadvantaged persons in the inner city. In March 1965, he responded to the call of Dr. Martin Luther King Jr. and participated in the civil rights march from Selma to Montgomery. A few years later in 1968, he participated in the Poor People's Campaign in Washington, DC, where he lived in Resurrection City for a few days and helped distribute food to the large crowd.

From 1989 to 2001, Bernie directed the Toledo diocesan Mission of Accompaniment to the BaTonga people in Zimbabwe. He visited the missionary team there six times and wrote a book about his experience, *Surprises of the Spirit*, which emphasizes the great generosity of the BaTongo people, despite bearing the cross of economic deprivation. During much of the last decade of his life, Bernie suffered from Parkinson's disease. He showed little interest in treating his illness but poured his heart into accepting his personal cross, which he did with great grace right up to his death.

Bernard Boff lived the Apostle Paul's teaching on the cross: continuing to preach the crucified Christ, even when inconvenient; maintaining a calm spirit in the face of criticism of his strong stands on social justice; reaching out to those bearing heavy crosses of deprivation and injustice; expanding his sphere of compassionate care to Africa; and accepting the crosses of daily life as preparation for accepting death as the passageway to eternal life.

What specific step could I take to more fully embrace the crosses of my life?

13. DEVELOPING A CHRISTOCENTRIC SPIRITUALITY

The Catholic tradition is a large complex symbol system with diverse doctrines, moral principles, and devotional practices. It is important to remember that all the elements of that very beautiful, diverse symbol system find their true meaning in relation to Jesus Christ. The beginning of the Apostle Paul's letter to the Romans, the longest and most theologically significant of his letters, clarifies this focus. It is addressed to the Christians in Rome, a community he did not establish but intends to visit. Paul introduces himself under three designations: a "slave" who glories in accepting Christ as his master, "an apostle" sent by the Lord to deliver a message, and as one "set apart" to preach "the gospel of God" (1:1).

For Paul, the gospel focuses on Jesus Christ, the son of King David according to the flesh and the Son of God established in power through the resurrection. It was the risen Christ who bestowed on Paul "the grace of apostleship" to bring "the obedience of faith" to all the Gentiles, including the "beloved of God" in Rome, who are "called to belong to Jesus Christ" and "to be holy." Paul completes his introduction with a prayer that God the Father and Jesus the Lord will grant the Christians in Rome the gift of grace and peace (Rom 1:5–7).

Let us explore what spiritual advice we can glean from the opening verses of Romans. Like Paul, we are called to make Christ central in our lives, serving him as our Master and sharing in his mission. A fifty-year-old cradle Catholic, who practiced his faith by carefully observing Church laws, made a retreat that transformed his Church-centered piety into a Christ-centered spirituality that includes a new personal relationship with the Lord and his call to serve those in need.

Paul had a core paschal spirituality based on the conviction that we are saved by the death and resurrection of Christ. God the Father raised the crucified Jesus to a new glorified life as the Son of God in power. A grandmother, who had a predominantly Good Friday piety centered on the intense suffering of Jesus, read comments by Pope Francis that helped her develop a more Easter-oriented spirituality focused on the joy of the resurrection.

The Apostle to the Gentiles reminds us that we are all called to be holy. By virtue of our baptism, we share in the life of Christ and in his mission to spread the kingdom in the world. The path to holiness passes through the area of our daily activities. When a single father of two grade school-age girls learned more about the universal call to holiness, he used his demanding parental duties to enrich his spiritual life, becoming more patient, tolerant, and prayerful.

What specific steps can I take to maintain a Christ-centered focus in my faith?

14. MINING THE RICHES OF THE CHRISTMAS LITURGY

Christmas remains a major religious celebration for Catholic families. Romans 16:25–27 prepares us for a more fruitful celebration of the Nativity of Christ. Written in preparation for his proposed visit to Rome, Paul concludes the letter with a prayer of praise to God that includes some of the major themes of his preaching. The prayer is expressed in one very long sentence with various clauses, making it difficult to decipher. In essence, Paul is offering praise and glory to "the only wise God" through Jesus Christ. From all eternity, God has had a plan to save and unify the whole human family. For "long ages" this plan remained secret, but it has been gradually revealed, first through the prophets and now, most fully, through "the proclamation of Jesus Christ." Paul preached the gospel of Christ, the good news of salvation, to "bring about the obedience of faith," which offers strength and fullness to people of "all nations."

We can view this passage from Romans as a commentary on the mystery of the incarnation celebrated on Christmas. As Christians, we believe in the one God who is the creator of the world, the sustainer of the historical process, and the final judge of all. From the very beginning, our God had a secret plan to save the whole human family. Israel kept alive the divine promise of salvation, especially through its great prophets such as Isaiah and Jeremiah. In the fullness of time, God sent his son into the world to establish the kingdom of justice and peace. As Son of God and son of Mary, Jesus, born in a stable and baptized by John, went about doing good, which aroused the fear and anger of the authorities who had him crucified. Obedient unto death, Christ was raised by his Father to a glorious life, becoming life-giving spirit for all and making the divine plan of salvation definitive and irrevocable. We Christians are called to bet our lives on Jesus Christ by committing ourselves to him and participating in his mission. In Romans, Paul prompts us to celebrate Christmas as a beautiful expression of our core Christian belief that Jesus fulfilled the divine promise of salvation for all.

We can imagine how a family attending Christmas Mass could be enlightened by Paul's instructions. The grandmother who thinks only Catholics are saved could realize that her Protestant, Jewish, and Muslim friends are also included in God's salvation plan. The father who attends Mass only on Christmas and Easter could decide to come more often, since he senses that it would help him better manage his stressful life. The mother who concentrates on keeping the Commandments could realize that her faith is more about generously following Christ than keeping rules. The teenage son who is struggling with feelings of inferiority could find some confidence in knowing that God loves him enough to send his Son into a troubled world. The grade school daughter who loves getting Christmas presents could remember it is Christ's birthday.

How can I get more out of the Christmas liturgy?

15. SUFFERING FOR FIDELITY TO THE GOSPEL

Does fidelity to Christ ever cause me any suffering or discomfort? In reflecting on that question let us consider 1 Peter 2:20–25. This epistle was probably originally addressed to Christian communities scattered throughout Asia Minor, for the most part modern-day Turkey. It seems these Christians were suffering in some way, probably not an official Roman persecution, but more likely the daily crosses of following Christ in a pagan culture. This passage encourages Christians to follow the example of Christ, the Suffering Servant, by suffering patiently for doing what is good. "This is a grace before God," a calling to walk in the footprints of Christ who suffered for us. The author goes on to describe the sufferings of Christ in the language of Isaiah 53:4–7, depicting the Suffering Servant. When Jesus, himself sinless, "was insulted, he returned no insult; when he suffered, he did not threaten;

instead, he handed himself over to the one who judges justly." Christ "bore our sins in his body upon the cross, so that, free from sin, we might live for righteousness."

We are called to pattern our lives after Christ the innocent victim, who submitted himself to the will of the Father and patiently suffered, without thoughts of vengeance, to free us from sin and strengthen us to live righteously. The passage concludes with a reference to Christ the shepherd, the "guardian of your souls," who brings back the straying sheep. This image not only comforts us in our failures to carry our crosses patiently but also reminds us of Christ who is the "gate" for the sheep who know his voice.

Suffering is built into human existence. Some of it is inevitable. Some of it is self-induced. There are other sufferings, however, that come our way because we are following Christ and living his gospel. The epistle urges us to bear this suffering patiently, as did Jesus.

We know people who follow Christ's example. Parents who persevere in setting limits on the cell phone use of their children despite constant pressure to allow free access. Prison inmates who continue to attend religious services despite the demeaning comments of other inmates. Collegians who maintain high standards of sexual morality despite being left out of some desirable social situations. White families who befriend their black neighbors despite incurring the displeasure of some of their white friends.

Do I experience any tension between my Christian faith and everyday life in the United States?

16. SERVING AS RECONCILERS

As Christians, we are called to carry on Christ's work of reconciling damaged relationships—often a challenging task. In 2 Corinthians 5:17–21, Paul develops the theme of reconciliation. Referring to himself, he declares that in Christ we are a new creation because God "has reconciled us to himself through Christ and given us the ministry of reconciliation." The Apostle identifies himself as an ambassador for Christ, entrusted with "the message of reconciliation," namely that God reconciled the world to himself in Christ. Paul then implores us to "be reconciled to God."

The English word *reconciliation* means "to restore to friendship or harmony." In Paul's letters it refers to God's initiative in and through Christ restoring our relationship with our Creator and Judge. Through baptism we are incorporated into Christ, becoming a new creation and sharing in his glorified life. Blessed with a loving friendship with God, we are called, like Paul, to be ambassadors for Christ, proclaiming the good news of salvation for all. We carry on our ministry of reconciliation in our daily lives by promoting harmony in our families, cooperation in the workplace, friendships in our neighborhoods, dialogue in our country, and peace in our world.

Reconciliation happens in personal relationships that are dynamic, subject to change and development. By his death and resurrection, Christ has achieved a definitive and irrevocable reconciliation of the human family with his ever-faithful Father. From our perspective, however, we are called to deepen and extend our relationship with God. We find inspiration in our fellow Christians who grow spiritually, deepen their prayer life, and intensify their commitment to serve God.

We know faithful individuals who have served as dedicated and effective ministers of reconciliation: the husband who demonstrated great perseverance and wisdom in successfully keeping his wife from giving up on their daughter during her troubled teenage years; the construction worker who served as a buffer between his white, prejudiced foreman and his black coworker friend; the grandmother who got two of her grandsons who were fighting over money to sit down and resolve their differences; the woman who got her estranged neighbors to work together on a block watch program, making the neighborhood a safer place to live; the pastoral administrator who talked her pastor into meeting with a disgruntled parishioner who wanted to vent her frustration over the limited role of women in the Church; the CEO of a medium-sized company who sponsored an annual conflict management seminar for all her employees; the idealistic young man who volunteered for the army as his way of serving his country and promoting peace in the world.

What specific thing could I do to become a better minister of reconciliation?

17. OVERCOMING ANTI-SEMITISM

Over the last few years there has been a very disturbing increase in hate crimes and verbal attacks on Jewish citizens of the United States. As Christians we have a responsibility to develop a positive attitude toward our Jewish sisters and brothers. A good starting point is Romans 9—11, which treats the role of the Jews in God's plan of salvation. Paul, himself a Pharisaic Jew, approaches the issue in a very personal way. Although his mission is by divine command directed to the Gentiles, he is saddened that his own people, the Jews, are rejecting Jesus as their promised Messiah. He is so distressed that he would be willing to sacrifice his own salvation for the sake of his fellow Israelites. Noting the "constant anguish" in his heart, Paul makes his point with graphic conviction: "For I could wish that I myself were accursed and separated from Christ for the sake of my [own people], my kin according to the flesh."

Paul goes on to recount the glories of his fellow Israelites, recalling in shorthand the major events in the history of

Israel: God making a covenant with Abraham, Moses leading the exodus from Egypt and receiving the Commandments on Mount Sinai, King David representing the promise of a Messiah, and Solomon building the temple for divine worship. Most important, the Israelite bloodline, going back to Abraham, produced Jesus, son of Joseph of the House of David, the Christ who is the King over all and God-blessed forever. Paul's anguish is sharpened because his people, prepared by God over the centuries for the Messiah, do not recognize Jesus, who exceeds all expectations. As Matthew 14:22–33 tells us, in his public ministry, Jesus himself had to deal with the lack of faith of his fellow Jews. For example, when Peter faltered while walking toward his Master on the water, Jesus chided him as having "little faith."

The passage from Romans raises many issues for discussion, but let us concentrate on the importance of recognizing the Jewishness of Jesus. He was the son of Jewish parents, learned the Hebrew Scriptures, celebrated the great feasts, visited the temple, went regularly to synagogue services, and celebrated a Passover meal with his disciples the evening before his execution. The evangelists presented him in terms taken from the Hebrew Scriptures: the Suffering Servant portrayed by Isaiah, the Son of Man mentioned in Daniel, a Wisdom figure greater than Solomon, the new Moses, the son of David, the prophet greater than Elijah, the promised Messiah, and the new center of worship replacing the temple. He said he came not to abolish the Jewish law but to fulfill it, and with few exceptions he limited his ministry to his fellow Jews.

We Christians can find common ground with our Jewish friends by remembering the Jewish context of the life and message of Jesus. An elderly Catholic with lingering thoughts of Jews as "God killers" could develop a more positive outlook on the great Jewish religious tradition shared by Christ. A regular participant in Sunday liturgy could put more attention on how the Old Testament reading complements the gospel. A high school religion teacher could put more emphasis on the Jewish roots of Jesus, for example, how he creatively combined the love of God and the love of neighbor taught in the Hebrew Scriptures. A parishioner who has strong convictions as to the divinity of Christ could come to a greater appreciation of his humanity by reflecting on his Jewish roots.

What can I do to help overcome anti-Semitism?

18. DEVELOPING A BALANCED PASCHAL SPIRITUALITY

It can be difficult for us Christians to keep a healthy perspective on the horrible sufferings and tragic death of Jesus on the cross. For example, Pope Francis has warned that it distorts our faith to make Good Friday more important than Easter. The magnificent hymn of Philippians 2:6–11 helps us keep a balanced approach to Christ's death and resurrection.

This hymn was probably composed by the early Christian community and inserted by Paul into his correspondence with his beloved Christian community in the Roman colony of Philippi. The hymn can be divided into two parts: the abasement of Christ and his exaltation. Christ Jesus, "though he was in the form of God,...emptied himself, taking the form of a slave, coming in human likeness." "He humbled himself, becoming obedient to death, even death on a cross." This is a powerful poetic expression of an essential Christian truth that we commonly designate with the abstract theological term *incarnation*.

The second part of the hymn stresses the exaltation of Christ: "Because of this, God greatly exalted him and bestowed on him the name that is above every name, that at the name of Jesus every knee should bend." This beautiful verse expresses the fundamental conviction of Christian faith, which we traditionally summarize in theological language as "resurrection and glorification." More than theological doctrines, this imaginative hymn has an intrinsic power to touch our hearts and shape our imaginations with the fundamental truth of the gospel.

Philippians also helps us interpret Christ's passion primarily as a story of obedience and not suffering. Jesus was not a masochist looking to suffer and die. He was a faithful servant committed to doing God's will, and his obedient fidelity brought him into conflict with the religious and political authorities, who conspired to execute him. Jesus suffered terribly, but this was a by-product of total dedication to the cause of God and humanity. Furthermore, the epistle reminds us that the burial of Jesus is not really the last word. Death leads to life; resurrection completes the story. Good Friday makes sense only when illumined by Easter. Jesus humbled himself even unto death and for this reason God exalted him.

We can imagine some personal responses to serious reflection on the Philippian hymn. A teacher: "I understand better why I was troubled by Mel Gibson's movie *The Passion of the Christ*; it centered so much on the horrible suffering of Jesus without giving any indication that it was a by-product of his obedience." A parishioner: "I have grown to appreciate the icon of the Risen Christ in our church—it completes the story of the fourteen stations, which ends with the burial." A mother: "I have always loved the Palm Sunday liturgy with the reading of the passion, but now I also see it as a preparation for a more joyful celebration of Easter." A collegian: "I am developing a more positive joyful spiritual life than the legalistic Catholicism I grew up with, and the poetry of the hymn helps me imagine new possibilities."

What do I need to do to maintain a balanced spirituality?

19. PRACTICING SELF-SACRIFICING LOVE

Our Christian faith teaches us that we are graced children of God but are threatened by sin and guilt. We know the temptation to act selfishly, to be overly concerned with our own welfare at the expense of others. Jesus Christ, by example and teaching, calls us to overcome this temptation and to practice self-sacrificing love.

In Philippians 2:6–11, the Apostle Paul introduces a beautiful traditional hymn by admonishing us to imitate Christ Jesus, who was "in the form of God," but "emptied himself, taking the form of a slave" and "humbled himself, becoming obedient to death, even death on a cross."

Paul's poetic description of Christ's abasement, with its power to touch the imagination, can be put in more theological language. Christ is true God of true God, one in being with the Father, the second person of the Blessed Trinity, the eternal Word. According to the Christian doctrine of the incarnation, the Word became flesh, the Son of God became human, fully embracing the human condition with its joys and sorrows. Jesus, who was like us in all things but sin, was born in a stable, lived for over thirty years in the small, nondescript village of Nazareth, had no permanent home during his itinerate public ministry, and lived his whole life in an occupied country impoverished by excessive taxation. He insisted to his disciples that he came not to be served but to serve others and reinforced this teaching by washing the feet of his disciples at the Last Supper, instructing them to follow his own example. He was indeed the Suffering Servant, who devoted his whole life to serving the cause of God and humanity, even to the point of death on the cross.

As Christians, we all have the obligation to adopt the attitude of Christ and to follow his example of self-sacrificing love. We can find inspiration in the example of good people: mothers who sacrifice their own interests and devote their lives to raising their children; doctors who go the extra mile in treating each of their patients with compassion and respect; members of the armed services who sacrifice their lives in serving the country; lawyers who do more than their share of pro bono service; fathers who work extra hours without complaint to support their families; secretaries who are patient and kind to people even when they do not feel like it; elected officials who vote their conscience despite opposition among their constituents; women religious who serve the needy without seeking acclaim; pastors who set aside their own needs in order to serve their parishioners; firemen who risk their lives to protect others; teachers who make financial sacrifices in order to teach in parochial schools; homebound people who put more time and energy into praying for others than complaining about their problems; young people who put their personal interests on hold while devoting themselves to social causes, such as gun control.

What next step could I take to follow the example of Christ who gave himself for me?

20. DEEPENING MY COMMITMENT TO CHRIST

The influential German Jesuit theologian Karl Rahner famously said, "I am a Christian in order to become one." As Christians, we are called to the ongoing process of deepening our faith in Jesus Christ. First John 5:1–6, probably written near the end of the first century by a member of the community dedicated to the Beloved Disciple, treats the issue of faith in Christ. The first verse declares, "Everyone who believes that Jesus is the Christ is begotten by God." The title "Christ," which means anointed one, came to be associated with the promised Jewish Messiah and was later applied by Christians to Jesus the risen Lord. Confessing Jesus as the Christ is to express belief in him as the fulfillment of the divine promise to save Israel.

Having faith in Jesus means we are begotten of God, made children of the Father, born into the divine family, formed into brothers and sisters of Christ. This close familial relationship grounds the command to love one another. Faith and love are intimately connected, forming a fruitful Christian life.

Later in the passage, the author reminds us that Jesus is not only the Messiah but also, and more fundamentally, the Son of God. The community of the Beloved Disciple had a high Christology, a strong sense of the divinity of Jesus as the Word made flesh. This faith enables Christians to conquer the world, which is subject to sin and darkness. Our faith in Christ, our personal relationship to him as Lord, empowers us to fight and defeat all the evil forces in the world. Furthermore, the passage suggests that belief has a trinitarian structure, including faith in God who is Father of all, Jesus who is Son of God, and the Holy Spirit who testifies to the truth.

What can we get out of prayerful reflection on this text and its insightful analysis of faith? Those who have a strong faith in Jesus as a wise teacher and preeminent moral guide could gain a better appreciation of Christ as the divine Son of God. Those who have a very private faith in Jesus the Savior could expand their faith by applying it to spreading the kingdom of justice and peace in the world. Those who have trouble accepting fellow Christians with a very different theology and piety could remember that they too are children of God, saved by Christ and animated by the Spirit. Those with a faith centered primarily on Christ could develop a deeper appreciation of the role of the Holy Spirit in a lively spirituality. We could all look for ways to integrate the virtues of faith and charity more effectively in our daily lives.

What concrete step can I take to deepen my faith in Jesus Christ?

21. APPRECIATING TRANSFIGURATION EXPERIENCES

Amid the tedious routines of daily life, we should be grateful for moments when the glorified Christ lifts our spirits and gladdens our hearts. Second Peter 1:16–19 speaks to this type of experience. This letter, perhaps written as late as AD 130 by an unknown representative (other than the author of 1 Peter) of the tradition of the apostle Peter, is cast in the form of a final instruction to various Christian communities, probably in Asia Minor, given by Peter before his death.

The passage presents Peter's personal witness to the transfiguration of Christ recounted in the Gospels. It begins with Peter defending himself against the charge that he preached "cleverly devised myths." The early Christians expected the Parousia, the victorious second coming of Christ, to occur soon. A century after the death of Jesus in the year 30, critics were scoffing at belief in the Parousia because the earliest apostles were long dead and Christ had failed to return. The author has Peter defend his teachings on the second coming by referencing his own experiences of the transfiguration. He was an eyewitness when "that unique declaration" came to Christ from God's "majestic glory": "This is my Son, my beloved, with whom I am well pleased." Linking himself with James and John, Peter testifies that they heard God's voice when they were on the mountain with Jesus. He goes on to insist that his prophetic teaching on the Parousia is "altogether reliable." The passage concludes with an admonition: "You will do well to be attentive" to this teaching on the second coming as "to a lamp shining in a dark place, until day dawns and the morning star rises in your hearts."

Later, in the third chapter of the epistle, the author defends belief in the Parousia by insisting that it was taught by Peter and other prophets and apostles and by claiming it is really not delayed, because it is subject to God's time, not ours. His main argument remains, however, the reliability of Peter who was an eyewitness to the transfiguration of the Lord.

Although the timing of the Parousia is an important issue for some Christian groups, most Christians today live their faith daily without great concern about the end of the world and a final judgment. On the other hand, there is interest in the coming of the Lord in the present moment, in meeting Christ in everyday life. We could say there is a hunger for transfiguration-type experiences that open our minds and hearts to the presence of Christ who reveals the glory of God.

It is not unusual to hear individuals give witness to such experiences. A social activist: "I was moved to tears when I listened again to Martin Luther King Jr.'s 'I Have a Dream' speech." A mom who worked two jobs to pay for her son's college education: "My heart almost burst with pride when that fine young man of mine walked on that stage and received his diploma." A happily married man: "There have been times when my beautiful wife and I made love and I felt close not only to her but also to God." A nature lover: "When I see the first flowers of spring my soul smiles with a renewed sense of hope."

What are my own most significant transfiguration experiences?

22. OVERCOMING CHRISTIAN DIVISIONS

Divisions have plagued the Christian community since the earliest days. Today we are more aware of rivalries not only between Catholics and Protestants but also within the Catholic Church. The Apostle Paul took on this serious problem in 1 Corinthians 1:10–17. About five years after he founded the Corinthian community in AD 51, Paul was told by associates of Chloe, a prominent female citizen, that rivalries had developed in the Church. It seems Christians were identifying exclusively with one or the other leader, Cephas (Peter), Apollos, or Paul himself. Paul makes the case for unity with a series of rhetorical questions. "Is Christ divided? Was Paul crucified for you? Or were you baptized in the name of Paul?" The Apostle to the Gentiles goes on to point out that Christ sent him to preach the gospel, not with "the wisdom of human eloquence," but with emphasis on the meaning of the cross of Christ. It seems that Paul is arguing that the way to bring various factions together is by concentrating on the essential gospel message of salvation through the crucified and risen Christ.

Corinthian factionalism has plagued the Church throughout its history. In 1054, the long-standing differences between Eastern and Western Christianity resulted in mutual excommunications, leaving us with the continuing split between the Roman Catholic and Eastern Orthodox Churches. The Protestant Reformation of the sixteenth century issued in the ongoing separation of Catholics and Protestants as well as hundreds of different Protestant denominations. Within the Catholic Church today we find disagreements between various groups, for example, between conservatives and progressives. Sometimes religious differences lead to polarization and demonization of opponents. In other situations, the differences foster dialogue that moves toward mutual respect and agreement on fundamental truths.

During his pontificate, Pope Francis has consistently centered his teaching and ministry on Jesus Christ and his law of love, especially his care for the poor and marginalized. This has grounded his efforts to promote ecumenical dialogue and cooperation.

At the grass roots, ordinary Christians follow the same Pauline strategy in coming together around fundamental convictions. A Catholic wife and Protestant husband, for instance, have maintained their marriage by going to Catholic Mass together on Saturday afternoon and to Protestant worship on Sunday morning. They share the common belief that Christ is truly present when two or three are gathered in his name. A conservative Catholic teacher befriended a progressive Catholic businessman after they collaborated on establishing a food distribution program for the poor in their parish—a friendship rooted in their shared belief that Christ calls us to feed the hungry.

What can I do to overcome divisions among Christians?

23. BUILDING UP THE BODY OF CHRIST

As baptized Christians, we are called to build up the Body of Christ. In 1 Corinthians 12:12–30, Paul uses the analogy of how the human body functions to urge a healthy unity in diversity for the divided church in Corinth. He begins, "As a body is one though it has many parts, and all the parts of the body, though many, are one body, so also Christ." The Apostle makes his general principle more specific: Even "if an ear should say, 'Because I am not an eye I do not belong to the body,'" it still does belong to the body. "If the whole body were an eye, where would the hearing be?" It makes no sense for the eye to say to the hand, "I do not need you." God constructed the human body with all its parts so that "there are many parts, yet one body," and "if [one] part suffers, all the parts suffer with it." Paul concludes with a brief reminder to his Corinthian converts that they are all members of Christ's Body and that some are designated as apostles, prophets, teachers, those who work mighty deeds, healers, administrators, and those who speak in tongues and interpret them.

We can view the passage as a catalyst for celebrating ways the Church today functions as the Body of Christ. By virtue of our baptism, we are all members of the Church, co-responsible for its well-being and its mission. We can celebrate the large number of Catholics who have recognized and embraced that role since Vatican II. In our contemporary world, the Church needs to model genuine unity in diversity that insists on holding in common fundamental truths (Christ is our risen Lord) and practices (regular celebration of the eucharistic liturgy), while allowing freedom in nonessentials (Marian devotions). Working this out in concrete challenging situations is extremely complex.

We can celebrate parishes that emphasize the preaching and practice the fundamentals of the faith while welcoming a wide variety of devotions. The Church is more credible when it teaches and practices the consistent ethic of life that protects and supports the most vulnerable: the unborn, the poor, the refugees and immigrants, the disabled, the elderly, and the dying. We can celebrate the pro-life groups that support pregnant women before and after birth as well as the social justice committees that in their efforts to assist the vulnerable include the unborn.

Ideally, parishes should promote harmony and teamwork among the parishioners and ministers. We can celebrate pastoral leaders who find ways to foster unity in diversity: encouraging parishioners to get involved, providing educational opportunities for parish ministers, respecting individual charisms, preaching the gospel so that over time everyone feels included in the message and no one feels excluded, encouraging parishioners to suggest new programs and approaches, involving parishioners in big decisions about parish life, and creating an atmosphere of trust that fosters cooperation for the good of the parish.

What specific thing could I do to build up the Body of Christ?

24. COOPERATING WITH CHRIST'S LIBERATING POWER

Authentic Christianity does not constrain or limit our freedom but liberates us for a full life of personal development and service to others. In Galatians 5:1–18, the Apostle Paul tells us, "For freedom Christ set us free; so stand firm and do not submit again to the yoke of slavery." As indicated by the context of this passage, Paul is contrasting Christian freedom won by Christ with the slavery of legalistic approaches to religious beliefs. Throughout the Letter to the Galatians, Paul insists salvation is from faith in Christ and not from observance of the Jewish law, a crucial teaching for the spread of Christianity in the first century but with limited relevance for us today. Paul goes on to make a point that does speak to us: "You were called for freedom," but "do not use this freedom as an opportunity for the flesh," for "the flesh has desires against the Spirit." For Paul, the "flesh" represents not just sexual sins, but all the inclinations of human nature that threaten our relationship with God and move us toward destructive, selfish behavior. Authentic freedom does not mean license to do whatever we want or to follow our unhealthy impulses.

More positively, the Apostle advises us that Christian freedom calls us to "serve one another through love," to love our neighbor as ourselves, and to "live by the Spirit," who guides and strengthens us to act for God and to follow the law of Christ.

According to Paul, Christ has freed us from all manner of constraints that inhibit our spiritual growth: for example, selfish tendencies; addictions to perceived pleasures, such as sex, drugs, shopping, gambling, and alcohol; neurotic guilt; excessive anxiety about personal salvation; exorbitant need for affirmation and praise; resentment and rage; the need to dominate and control; irrational fears; compulsive work habits; and anything of preliminary importance that becomes an absolute concern. The Christian claim is not that faith in Christ automatically liberates us from all such constraints, but that divine grace, which empowers our cooperation, is more powerful than the enslaving forces.

The Apostle also teaches us that Christ has freed us for doing good: for practicing love of neighbor, for spreading the reign of justice and peace in our world, and for responding generously to the promptings of the Holy Spirit.

We recognize the liberating power of Christ in individuals who have overcome constraints and moved toward greater spiritual maturity: those who have overcome addictions and are helping others to follow a similar path; those who have overcome workaholic tendencies and are more loving spouses; those who have overcome selfish tendencies and devote themselves to helping those in need; those who have overcome fears of damnation and are more trusting of God's mercy; those who have overcome a narrow private piety and are engaged in the cause of justice and peace.

What specific step could I take to cooperate more effectively with Christ's liberating power?

25. LEARNING FROM CHRIST OUR HIGH PRIEST

The New Testament presents us with many diverse images of Jesus Christ who walked our earth two thousand years ago, including common favorites such as the Good Shepherd and the Son of God. In our ongoing quest to deepen and expand our understanding of Christ, let us consider the Letter to the Hebrews, which develops the theme of Christ our high priest by comparing him favorably to the long line of Jewish high priests descended from Aaron. Those priests did not assume the honor themselves but were called by God as members of one of the divinely established priestly families. "Every high priest is taken from among men" to represent the people before God, offering "gifts and sacrifices for sins." High priests are able "to deal patiently with the ignorant and erring" because they themselves are "beset by weakness" and must make "sin offerings" for themselves as well as the people. The author concludes with one point of comparison, insisting that Christ did not glorify himself by becoming the high priest but received this honor from God his Father (Heb 5:1–6).

We are free to draw other lessons: for example, that Christ is one of us, aware of our weaknesses; that he represents us before God; that he offers sacrifices for our sins; and that he deals patiently with our ignorance and erring. This implicit message is good news for all of us as we contend with our sins, failures, mistakes, and limitations. Christ the eternal priest accompanies us as we walk the dark valley, carrying the full weight of our graced but sinful humanity. He is patient with us as we struggle to overcome our ignorance and to correct our mistakes. He is our mediator as we seek God's forgiveness for our sins and divine help for our spiritual journey.

Prayerful reflection on Christ our high priest could prompt some of us to take constructive steps to overcome our ignorance and mistakes. A woman shadowed by guilt over aborting her baby years ago could participate in Project Rachel, designed to facilitate forgiveness and healing. A father newly aware of the way his verbal abuse has hurt his teenage daughter could apologize and promise to be a more affirming father. A bachelor ashamed of objectifying women could make a conscious effort to treat his female colleagues and friends with greater respect. A woman conscious of her white privilege could do more to heal racial tensions in her neighborhood. A high school religion teacher handicapped by an outdated theology could consult the Catholic *Catechism* on questions that arise in class. An army veteran plagued with suicidal thoughts could seek professional help.

What next step could I take to grow in knowledge and practice of my faith?

26. CULTIVATING THE VIRTUE OF HOPE

As Christians, the hope that sustains us in challenging times is based on belief in Christ, our Savior. Hebrews 7:23–28 explores this connection. This passage begins by emphasizing the superiority of the priesthood of Christ over the Jewish

Levitical priesthood. While the Jewish priests were replaced after their death, Jesus, "because he remains forever, has a priesthood that does not pass away." He is always able to save us because "he lives forever to make intercession" for us.

The articulate unknown author goes on to insist that Christ, who is "holy, innocent, undefiled," had no need to offer many sacrifices, as did the Jewish priests, because "he did that once for all" by offering himself on the cross. The passage concludes by noting that the Jewish high priests were subject to "weakness," but that in the new era God appointed his Son Jesus Christ as the eternal priest "made perfect forever."

Let us reflect on the teaching of Hebrews that Jesus saved us by his life of fidelity to his Father that led to his passion and death. God raised the crucified Christ to a new glorified life, seating him at his right hand where he continuously intercedes for us. The ultimate triumph of good over evil is now ensured. The seeds of the final victory have been planted. God's will to save all people is now definitive and irrevocable. The eternal high priest has given us an invaluable gift, a grounded hope that divine grace is more powerful than all the satanic powers that assail us.

Christian hope provides a healthy perspective for dealing with both personal and social issues. It protects us against a skeptical cynicism that is overwhelmed by evil and paralyzed by doubt. Hope in the ultimate triumph of divine grace can alert us to the small victories of good over evil in our personal and public lives. It can encourage us to cooperate with Christ our high priest in his ongoing mission to humanize the world.

Today, we are in desperate need of the virtue of hope that prompts faithful efforts to overcome evil and promote the good. As citizens of the world, hope prompts us to oppose war and violence and to work for justice and peace. As Americans, hope prompts us to reject the tribal politics that divide us and to seek the common ground that unites us. As Christians, hope prompts us to avoid disparaging other religions and to collaborate with them in the great cause of world peace. As Catholics, hope prompts us to avoid despair over the sex abuse scandal and to do whatever we can to assist victims, to call perpetrators to account, and to prevent future abuse. As neighbors, hope prompts us to avoid excluding others and to find ways to welcome them. As parishioners, hope prompts us to avoid demonizing those who have opposing views and to take steps to learn from them for the good of the parish. As family members, hope prompts us to avoid harboring resentment and to seek reconciliation.

What concrete step could I take to practice the virtue of hope inspired by Christ our high priest?

27. SHARING IN THE MISSION OF CHRIST

As we look for realistic ways of participating in the mission of Christ, it might be helpful to examine the theological perspective found in chapter 9 of the Letter to the Hebrews (vv. 24–28), which portrays Christ as our eternal high priest, superior in various ways to the Jewish high priests. Presenting Christ as a priest is itself unusual since the historical Jesus was a Galilean layman who had no direct connections to the Jerusalem priestly families and was at times critical of temple practices.

This passage speaks about the "once for all" sacrificial death of Christ on the cross, contrasting this unique, unrepeatable event with the sacrifices offered every year by the Jewish high priests on the Day of Atonement. The passage goes on to state that Christ, who "offered once to take away the sins of many, will appear a second time, not to take away sin but to bring salvation to those who eagerly await him."

The Synoptic Gospels call this second appearance the *Parousia*, a Greek word indicating that the Son of Man will accomplish the final victory of good over all the evil powers at the end-time. In the Nicene Creed, we affirm that Christ "will come again in glory to judge the living and the dead." The whole historical process will reach its appointed goal when Christ completes his saving mission. The evolving world will share in the victory achieved by Christ. It is not for us to know the day or hour of this triumph, but our faith teaches that it will indeed happen in God's good time.

The language of "second coming" or "Christ's return" may be misleading since our risen high priest has never left us but has always been present as our mediator. We come closer to the meaning of the Parousia by seeing it as the completion of his ongoing mission to reconcile all things, making God "all in all."

This interpretation helps to make the doctrine more meaningful for us today. It reminds us that we share in Christ's mission now, in our everyday lives. We may not be much concerned about the Parousia or when it will occur, but we can put more effort into furthering the ongoing work of Christ to spread God's reign in the world.

We know good people who prepare for the Parousia just by meeting their daily responsibilities. The single mother who works full time to make a better life for her two children. The father who gives priority to the needs of his family despite the heavy demands of his job. The grandparents who raise the children of their deceased daughter. The coach who teaches her players that teamwork is more important than individual success. The teacher who spends extra time with troubled students. The nun who dedicates herself to prison ministry. The busy executive who does extra volunteer work in the community. The gay man who is especially attentive to his nieces and nephews. The citizen who votes intelligently. The collegian who develops good study habits. The priest who works hard at preparing his Sunday homily.

What can I do to contribute more to the ongoing mission of Christ?

28. PREPARING TO MEET CHRIST IN DAILY LIFE

Our Christian faith assures us that Christ has kept his promise not to abandon us. We make our life journey with the Lord as our constant companion. This reality makes it imperative that we stay attentive to Christ's abiding presence and remain responsive to his guidance and encouragement. Although the fifth chapter of 1 Thessalonians concentrates on Christ's second coming, it also reminds us of Christ's coming to us now (vv. 1–6).

It seems the Thessalonians were very concerned about the scheduling of the Parousia (the second coming of the Lord), wanting to know exactly when Christ would return to complete his mission and what signs would warn them of this "day of the Lord." In our passage, Paul tells them they do not need instruction on this for "the Lord will come like a thief at night." For those in darkness who are blinded by a false sense of "peace and security," the return of Christ will come like a "sudden disaster," bringing suffering like the pains of a woman in labor. On the other hand, believers, like the Thessalonians, who are "children of the light" have nothing to fear from the "day of the Lord," whenever it occurs, as long as they follow his admonition, "let us not sleep as the rest do, but let us stay alert and sober."

CONVERSION AS A WAY OF LIFE

What meaning does this passage have for us today, two millennia after Paul wrote it in response to real concerns of his early Christian community? For one thing, it reminds us that belief in the Parousia is an essential part of Christian faith as expressed in the Nicene Creed: "He will come again in glory to judge the living and the dead, and his kingdom will have no end." For most contemporary Christians, however, the timing of the Parousia is not of great personal concern.

Another way to make this teaching relevant is to concentrate on growing spiritually by being more alert to the ways we encounter Christ in our everyday activities. We believe Christ is present in all the people we meet: family, friends, colleagues, parishioners, strangers, and enemies. Our days are filled with opportunities to share personally in Christ's mission to spread the reign of God. A healthy prayer life can help us stay alert to potential encounters with the Lord.

Every day while driving to work, Ted asks God to give him the strength and wisdom to deal charitably with an egocentric coworker who talks incessantly about himself and his accomplishments. June spends fifteen minutes in meditation each morning, which enables her to interact more effectively with her three children, each one with unique gifts and challenges. John leaves Mass each Sunday determined to see Christ in someone he meets that week, with special attention to individuals in need. Lydia, a lifelong Catholic, made a life-transforming retreat that taught her that her religion was not primarily about keeping laws but about heeding Christ's call to love God by loving the neighbor who crosses her path.

How can I be more alert to finding Christ in my everyday activities?

29. RELYING ON CHRIST'S GRACE

It has been said that original sin is the one empirically verifiable Christian doctrine. Indeed, we have experience of the distortions built into the human condition and the glamour of evil lurking in our own hearts. Paul's long letter to the Christians in Rome, a community he did not found but intended to visit, contains the classic text for the later development of the doctrine of original sin as well as the doctrine of salvation by Christ (Rom 5:12–19).

In that passage, Paul makes a comparison between Adam and Christ. Adam brought sin into the world, which affected all people, making us all subject to death. Paul makes his point in this way: "Through one person sin entered the world, and through sin, death, and thus death came to all." He insists, however, that the gift of salvation won for us by Christ is more powerful than the sin of Adam. "For if by that one person's transgression the many died, how much more did the grace of God and the gracious gift of the one person Jesus Christ overflow for the many." Christ inaugurated a new era of grace, making salvation available to all people and definitively ensuring that grace is always and everywhere more powerful than sin and death.

Historically, this passage was used as the basis for gradually developing the doctrine of original sin, which does not refer to personal sin or collective guilt, but is a way of describing the flawed character of the human condition and our own experience of the tendency to ignore our best impulses and to follow our worst inclinations. In that constant struggle, we can be confident that Christ's grace is always stronger than the threat of sin.

We can all find inspiration in famous individuals who persevered in their faith commitment based on that Christian conviction: Mother Teresa, Óscar Romero, Nelson Mandela, Martin

Luther King Jr., and Dorothy Day. We can also find encouragement in people we know: a social activist who has maintained her work for prison reform over many decades despite not seeing much progress; the husband who remained committed to his wife despite her many debilitating illnesses; the vowed religious who maintained a hopeful spirit through the Vatican investigation of American religious orders; a faithful citizen who decides to stay active politically despite extreme disappointment over recent elections.

Does my belief that Christ's grace is more powerful than sin make any difference in my life?

30. PERSEVERING IN THE CHRISTIAN LIFE

In our effort to persevere in living as committed Christians, we find encouragement in the twelfth chapter of Hebrews (vv. 1–4): "Since we are surrounded by so great a cloud of witnesses, let us rid ourselves of every burden and sin that clings to us and persevere in running the race that lies before us while keeping our eyes fixed on Jesus, the leader and perfecter of faith." The passage invites us to imagine ourselves in a large stadium with a big crowd cheering us on as we run a long-distance race. Thinking of our life on this earth as a race suggests that it has a finish line created by death, that it is possible to get tired and give up, that sin slows us down, and that there is a reward for finishing the race that we call heaven. The "cloud of witnesses" includes those who have already completed the race and now serve as inspiring examples and effective intercessors on our behalf. Sin slows our pace by diverting our attention from the true God, weakening our resolve, distorting our priorities, and creating the illusion that life is a rat race without ultimate meaning.

We can counter sin by keeping our eyes on Christ, our leader, who ran a perfect race, enduring the cross and transforming its shame into the joy of his risen life at the right hand of the Father. During his own race on this earth, Jesus "endured such opposition from sinners," in order that we "may not grow weary and lose heart" during our earthly race.

As Christians, we know something of our need for Christ's help as we struggle to live our faith in everyday life. A single mother raising two kids and working a strenuous full-time job asks Christ at Mass every Sunday to give her energy to make it through one more week. A corporate executive committed to controlling his anger at work spends a few minutes before heading to the office reflecting on the patience of Christ dealing with his disciples. An idealistic collegian tempted to give up on the whole messy political process maintains her commitment to faithful citizenship after an extended reflection on the words of Jesus in the garden: "Not my will but yours be done" (Luke 22:42). A middle-aged married man with a history of infidelity encounters Christ in the sacrament of reconciliation and renews his commitment to make his marriage work. A grandmother depressed by the death of her husband finds new energy by imitating Christ and being extra attentive to her grandchildren.

Can I recall a time when Christ helped me persevere in the fatiguing race of life?

31. FOCUSING ON CHRIST

The Catholic tradition includes a rich mix of doctrinal teachings, moral principles, liturgical celebrations, and devotions. As we try to maintain an integrated understanding of this vast symbol system, a passage from 2 Timothy, framed as an encouraging message from the Apostle Paul to his younger coworker, Timothy, prompts us to "remember Jesus Christ, raised from the dead, a descendent of David" (2:8–13). As followers of Christ, we confess that he is the promised son of the great King David, the long-awaited Messiah, who will establish God's reign in the world, a kingdom of justice and peace that will last forever. Obedient to the will of God, even to the point of death on the cross, Christ was raised to a new, eternal, and glorious life by his heavenly Father. The passage indicates that Paul is suffering greatly for proclaiming this gospel, the core of the good news of salvation. He is a Roman citizen but is in prison chained like a common criminal. He may be chained but "the word of God is not chained," suggesting its explosive power to break through all human barriers on its saving mission.

The passage also has Paul declaring, "Therefore, I bear with everything for the sake of those who are chosen, so that they too may obtain the salvation that is in Christ Jesus, together with eternal glory." He is willing to endure prison as part of his mission to proclaim to the Gentile world the salvation won by Christ. The Apostle then adds this "trustworthy" saying: "If we have died with him we shall also live with him; if we persevere we shall also reign with him."

We can hear this passage as a reminder to concentrate on the core message of our Christian faith. Christianity is not first a series of disparate truths to be believed or a collection of legal precepts to be followed. It is, rather, a commitment to a person, Jesus Christ, the Word of God made flesh, who went about doing good, which incurred the wrath of the powerful, who crucified him only to have God raise him to life and exalt him forever. Christ is himself the good news, the fullness of divine truth, the perfect respondent to divine love, the exemplar of human fulfillment, the mediator between

God and the human family. Christian doctrines, developed and declared over the centuries, illumine some aspect of this essential mystery of Christ. The Church's moral teachings, sometimes complex and disputed, serve as guidelines for living our commitment to Christ and following his law of love. The Christian tradition, with its marvelous diversity of saints, devotions, and practices, functions best when it focuses our attention on Christ's life and teachings.

We can imagine Catholics who can benefit from this christocentric focus of their faith. Those who find it hard to understand and accept some particular Church doctrines could concentrate on deepening their relationship to Christ, while staying open to the possibility that the questionable doctrines may one day enrich their spiritual life. Those who in good conscience cannot accept the Church's teaching on a specific issue, such as birth control, could continue to follow Christ's law of love in their daily life. Those tempted to leave the Catholic Church because of the sex abuse scandal could decide to stay, trusting that Christ will eventually guide the Church to genuine repentance and effective reform.

In what concrete way could a christocentric focus facilitate my spiritual growth?

32. FACING OUR SINFULNESS

As we seek healthy ways of dealing with our personal sinfulness, we find in 1 Timothy 1:12–17 an instructive example of the Apostle Paul as a model repentant sinner. The passage has Paul confess that he "was once a blasphemer and a persecutor and an arrogant man," and yet Christ treated him mercifully, considered him trustworthy, and appointed him to the ministry. In Paul, who acted out of ignorance, the grace of Christ has been an abundant source of faith and love. The passage concludes with Paul, who sees himself as a "foremost" sinner, enunciating a fundamental gospel truth: "Christ Jesus came into the world to save sinners."

It is indeed crucial to our spiritual growth and Christian practice to accept this fundamental truth. Refusing to admit sinfulness or even talk about it leaves us prey to repressed guilt feelings or hidden rationalizations. On the other hand, excessive preoccupation with guilt and sin can distort our Christian perceptions, turning God into a harsh judge, Christ into a masochist, and the Christian life into an anxious struggle to avoid mortal sins.

We can avoid these distortions by placing our real sinfulness in a more positive context. Our God is a merciful Father who never tires of forgiving us. Christ shared fully in our human existence, like us in all things except sin. Through his freely accepted self-sacrificing death and glorious resurrection, he has given us life, an abundant life filled with opportunities for spiritual growth and loving service. The harsh reality, however, is that we sometimes miss those opportunities: disappointing ourselves, failing to love as Christ taught us, hurting other people, shirking our responsibilities, opting for expediency over principle, settling for mediocrity, ignoring the common good, acting selfishly, and failing to challenge injustice and violence. In truth, we are sinners. The good news is that we are not imprisoned in our sinfulness. God's mercy, mediated by Christ, provides us with a way out, a path forward, a new beginning, divine forgiveness. Our calling is to follow the example of the Apostle Paul by expressing gratitude for forgiveness, working at reparation, and living the law of love.

We can find inspiration in other repentant sinners: murderers who reconcile with relatives of their victims, unfaithful spouses who become more loving marriage partners, racists who become advocates for social justice, authoritarian pastors who become true servant leaders, cynical citizens who become active in electoral politics, negligent friends who become attentive to others, drug addicts who become recovering integrated persons, disruptive parishioners who become team players, all those who have been blessed by God's mercy and have responded by becoming more virtuous persons.

In what specific way could I become a better repentant sinner?

33. RELYING ON CHRIST IN LIFE AND DEATH

As we strive to make Christ the decisive person in our lives and to open our minds and hearts to his message, we do well to reflect on Romans 14:7–9. There Paul reminds us that we are not isolated individuals but are essentially social beings, constituted by personal relationships. The Apostle puts it this way: "None of us lives for oneself, and no one dies for oneself." As Christians, we recognize that our most fundamental relationship is with Christ both in life and in death. The Apostle reminds us, "Whether we live or die, we are the Lord's." Through his death and resurrection, Christ was manifested as the Lord of both the living and the dead.

How can this short passage from Romans guide and enrich our spiritual journey? The Apostle insists that we do not thrive alone. Even when we walk in the dark valley of estrangement and isolation, Christ is at our side as a fellow traveler. Jill, who never found a suitable life partner, has enjoyed a happy and fulfilled life, sustained by her friends and her faith that Christ has been her constant companion.

Furthermore, Paul assures us that the Lord who illumines our path during our earthly sojourn also accompanies us as we make the passage through death into a life of eternal happiness. Pete, an engineer, who has no doubt Christ is with him in his everyday life, cannot wrap his mind around the whole concept of heaven and eternal life. Perhaps he could deal better with his doubts by concentrating on the fundamental truth that death will not destroy his relationship with Christ.

The epistle encourages us to accept Christ as our Lord and to live all aspects of our lives under his authority. Some Christians are open and explicit about Christ's role in their lives. Ellen, who has a close personal relationship to Jesus, is always ready to give witness to the role Christ plays in her life. Other Christians are less certain about their relation to Christ and more reluctant to speak about it. For example, Ellen's husband, Dan, was reluctant to talk to her about spiritual matters because he did not have the kind of personal relationship with Christ that she did. Dan became more open and vocal, however, when he recalled that Christ's teachings really do guide his business decisions. His piety is quite different from his wife's, but Christ still functions as Lord of his life.

Do I view Christ as Lord of my life and death?

34. TRUSTING CHRIST OUR MEDIATOR

As we strive to live as faithful Christians in challenging situations, we can find encouragement in the Letter to the Hebrews (4:14–16), an often underappreciated but theologically rich resource for understanding and living our Christian faith. The author assures us that in Jesus, the Son of God, "we have a great high priest who has passed through the heavens." In Israelite ritual, the high priest once a year passed through a curtain and incensed the holy of holies, where he sprinkled sacrificial blood on the mercy seat, the dwelling place of God. The passage encourages us to "hold fast" to our beliefs, because Christ, who is far superior to the Jewish high priests, continues to intercede for us.

The reading goes on to make the strongest explicit biblical affirmation of the full humanity of Christ: "For we do not have a high priest who is unable to sympathize with our weaknesses, but one who has similarly been tested in every way, yet without sin." Jesus Christ is true God and true man; he knows our joys and sorrows; he was tempted as are we, but always remained faithful. Representing all of us before God, he has reconciled us to our heavenly Father. "So let us confidently approach the throne of grace," as the epistle concludes, "to receive mercy and to find grace for timely help."

The passage invites reflection on our fundamental attitude toward God, our Creator, Redeemer, and Judge. It rules out a paralyzing fear of a harsh God who is ready to consign us to hell for even slight transgressions. On the other hand, it is misguided to presume that God is like a kindly grandfather who dotes on his grandchildren and consistently excuses their bad behavior. The God proclaimed by Christ is both a merciful father and a just judge.

Those drifting along, satisfied with mediocrity, prone to rationalize evil behavior, do well to recall that we are all accountable to the God who calls us to strive for the high ideals of the gospel. Those suffering from scrupulosity, anxiety over damnation, spiritual timidity, and excessive fear of divine wrath can benefit from reflecting on the compassionate God who loves us unconditionally and forgives us endlessly. We can approach God confidently because Christ, our high priest, who sits at the right hand of God the Father, continues to intercede for us, offering us the help we need to take the next constructive step on our spiritual journey.

We can imagine individuals encouraged by the intercession of Christ finding the confidence to ask God for the specific grace they need. A successful financial consultant who has drifted away from the Church could ask God to guide her back to a fuller expression of her Catholic faith. An elderly grandfather who spends sleepless nights rerunning memories of his minor faults and failings could petition God for the gift of a peaceful heart and a good conscience. A teacher who finds little consolation in prayer could seek the grace to persevere in her daily prayers despite God's silence. A salesman who is overly critical of his black customers could pray for the grace to overcome his prejudice.

What specific assistance should I seek from Christ the Mediator?

35. RELYING ON CHRIST OUR BROTHER

We all have favorite images of Christ that guide our prayer and practice of the faith. Sometimes new unfamiliar images can spark renewed spiritual energy. Let us turn to the Letter to the Hebrews, a carefully constructed, theologically insightful witness to Christ our high priest. The unknown author tells us that "for a little while" Christ was made "lower than the angels" so that "he might taste death for everyone." In the plan of God, "for whom and through whom all things exist," Jesus, our brother and leader, was willing to suffer so that we might attain glory (2:9–11).

The Letter to the Hebrews begins with a series of scripture quotes demonstrating the superiority of Christ over the angels and highlighting the importance of remaining faithful to the Lord in difficult times. It argues that in God's plan it was essential that Christ become "lower than the angels" for a time so that he could serve as our savior. In other words, Christ had to become human in order to share fully in human existence, including suffering and death. The incarnation is a necessary part of God's plan to save us. We are saved because one of us, the Word made flesh, who shared totally in our human condition, was obedient to death on the cross and was raised to life by his heavenly Father. Christ is true God, superior to the angels, and true man, fully sharing our human nature.

Historically, Christians have at times found it difficult to accept the full humanity of Christ. Some, known theologically as Docetists, have denied that he really suffered or had a true human nature or a real human will. Even today, it is hard for some Christians to accept that Jesus grew in knowledge, experienced human emotions, prayed to his Father, or went to his death in darkness. This passage from Hebrews calls us to accept Christ as one of us, our elder brother who truly suffered and died for us. Fully affirming Christ's humanity enables us to see him as a brother who understands our intellectual, emotional, and spiritual struggles. We can turn to him, confident that he knows our hearts and hears our prayers.

We can envision Christians who could benefit from reflection on Christ's human journey. A mother troubled by periodic conflicts with her teenage son could reflect on the conflict that the twelve-year-old, coming-of-age Jesus had with his parents. An elderly man who fears the isolation of dying could prayerfully consider the cry of Jesus on the cross, "Father, why have you forsaken me?" A woman with a strong devotion to Mary as her empathetic sister could broaden her spiritual life by considering Christ as her compassionate brother. A grad student frustrated with his slow progress on his dissertation could ponder the significance of Luke's statement that Jesus grew not only in age but also in wisdom. A community organizer discouraged by a lack of progress could meditate on Jesus who was misunderstood by religious and political authorities.

What aspect of Christ's humanity speaks to my own struggles?